PREFACI

D*aily Imperfections* (364 surprising and delightful "info-mations"—one, more or less, for each day of the year) is the imperfect offspring of its popular parent, *The Joy of Imperfection*. We wrote it for readers who clamored for more—more insight, more silliness, more assurance that we and the world around us are less than perfect. We wrote it because we know nothing about efficient allocation and management of time and resources. We wrote it because we play well with others and do not run with scissors.

Daily Imperfections proclaims that our sparkling defects and inevitable mistakes may be our most interesting and charming characteristics. Ordinary affirmations often teach us to ignore this truth, to deny who and how we really are. *Daily Imperfections* honors the lumps and bumps, flaws and failings, that make us simply human, normal, no weirder than the next guy. Perhaps they are our gifts to future generations.

The daily imperfections are divided into two types: those tied to specific dates and those not. The latter type highlights some of the speed bumps on the highway of life: relationship downsizing, the high cost of money, workplace blues, yard envy, gaining weight, and losing ground. Peer backwards or peek ahead and choose any one at any time as a distraction, a consolation, a bonbon to sweeten the day.

The former type commemorates strange events (the Deming Duck Race), historical anniversaries (Millard Filmore's birthday), or natural phenomena (the summer and winter solstices). Although tied to specific dates, these "info-mations" can be read randomly. Why not? We chose them because, if someone, somewhere, celebrates, we can all celebrate.

Daily Imperfections aims to question authority and highlight the arbitrary foolishness of the world we live in. Celebrating the date the first cow was milked in an airplane is no more foolish than celebrating April Fool's Day. *Daily*

Imperfections also expands our notion of historical truth. For example, it commemorates Matthew A. Henson, Admiral Robert E. Peary's valet and fellow explorer, who really got to the North Pole first. It spotlights common people and obscure events and gives them their nanosecond of fame. Feel free to insert your own achievements and toast your own small triumphs.

Take one daily imperfection, one one-a-day vitamin, and one day at a time. Enjoy.

DAILY IMPERFECTIONS

January 1

PERFECT BEGINNINGS

You're expected to be perfect the day you start and then improve.
—Ed Vargo

Perfectionists believe you're supposed to know it all before you learn it. You're supposed to do things before you know how, to make no mistakes, to read people's minds, and to be an expert without needing to practice. And—you're supposed to improve.

This year I resolve to honor and celebrate my sparkling imperfections.

January 2

HISTORIC BLOOPERS

Goof-ups can lead to unexpected and far-out destinations.
—Enid Howarth and Jan Tras

On this historically imperfect day in 1959, the first Soviet moon shot, LUNA 1, missed its target. LUNA 1 accidentally became the first spacecraft from earth to orbit the sun. Good shot. Wrong target.

Today I will shoot for the moon and be happy if I get near the sun.

January 3

LASTING ROMANCE

To love one's self is the beginning of a life-long romance.
                                                    –Oscar Wilde

Few relationships and even fewer romances last forever. Fortunately, it's never too late to fall in love with yourself. To do this you will have to accept, appreciate, and embrace all your delightful imperfections. Ain't love grand?

Today I will commit to life-long romance and live
happily ever after with you-know-who.

January 4

BOTTOMS UP

I've worked myself up from nothing to a state of extreme poverty.
                                                    –Groucho Marx

You may not be rich. You may not have everything or even enough. But you do have more than nothing. And more than nothing is something.

Today I will remember that my sluggish cash flow
is better than no flow at all.

January 5

JUST DESSERTS

If I only had a little humility I would be perfect.
−Ted Turner

No matter what you do, you'll never get to perfect from here. Even a little humility now and then won't get you there. Give up the struggle. You're already imperfect without even trying.

Today I'll eat humble pie and enjoy my just desserts.

January 6

DOWN FOR THE COUNT

Every man's got to figure to get beat sometime.
−Joe Louis

Nobody wins every time. You're lucky if you win sometimes. You've been very lucky.

I may be down today, but don't count me out.

January 7

POINTLESS POLITICS

When I was a boy, I was told that anybody could become president;
I'm beginning to believe it.

−Clarence Darrow

Millard Fillmore, bland 13th president of the United States, was born on this date in 1800. Overlooked even by his party, he ran for re-election as a candidate of the Know-Nothing Party in 1856 and lost. Today is an occasion to celebrate things boring and banal.

Today I will remember Millard and celebrate my lackluster career.

January 8

DESTROYING THE EVIDENCE

If at first you don't succeed, destroy all evidence that you tried.

−Author Unknown

You tried. You failed. It's time to shred the paperwork, wipe off the fingerprints, cover your tracks, hide the bodies. Only you know who done it. Don't tell.

Today I will make my comedy of errors into a Hitchcockian thriller.

January 9

FRIENDS INDEED

Friends help you move. Real friends help you move bodies.
–Author Unknown

You know someone is a real friend when they volunteer to help with the nasty stuff: cleaning the garage, burying the dog, undoing the sink trap to look for a ring, unclogging the toilet, listening to you complain. Real friends love you and share the consequences of your inadequacies and imperfections.

Today I will appreciate my real friends and offer
to help them do something awful.

January 10

MATURE IGNORANCE

I am not young enough to know everything.
–James M. Barrie

Once upon a time, you thought you knew everything. Life seemed simple, clear, and uncomplicated. Then you grew up.

Today I will be grateful that I am mature and don't know everything.

January 11

PACE MAKING

My doctor recently told me that jogging could add years to my life.
I think he was right. I feel ten years older already.
—Milton Berle

In the beginning, exercise hurts like hell. In the middle and at the end, it still hurts like hell. It makes you ache, sweat, feel perfectly righteous, and very old. It's the nature of exercise.

Today I will only keep pace with my rapidly advancing years.

January 12

BETTER LATE THAN BORING

I've been on a calendar, but never on time.
—Marilyn Monroe

You've been late, very late, for some very important dates. Perhaps you are forgetful, overbooked, accident-prone, or just very fashionable. Maybe you just hate to be early. Punctuality as a virtue is highly overrated.

Today I will move at my own pace and be happy
if I can remember what day it is.

January 13

THERE'S THE RUB

All marriages are happy. It's the living together
afterward that causes all the trouble.
—Raymond Hull

Living together through all of life's changes is a heroic task, not designed for the faint of heart. In the beginning, you hardly noticed the grains of sand in your shoe. After twenty years, those same shoes are full of sand, and every step is a challenge. Life's a beach.

Today I will remember how I first loved those old shoes.

January 14

HAVING FUN YOUR WAY

Most of the time I don't have much fun.
The rest of the time I don't have any fun at all.
—Woody Allen

If you're not having fun yet, you're probably feeling profoundly disappointed. That's okay. Disappointment might be your own special way of having fun.

Today I'll entertain myself by kvetching, complaining,
and lamenting my fate.

January 15

SWINGING ON THE FOOD CHAIN

Both the cockroach and the bird could get along very well without us,
although the cockroach would miss us most.
—Joseph Wood Krutch

You are a crucial link in the great chain of life. You are invaluable to the maintenance of ecological balance. Your very presence on the planet takes care of someone or something lower on the food chain. You are vital and deeply appreciated by beings whose names you don't even know.

Today I will try not to think about all the unseen creatures
I've been feeding and supporting.

January 16

NATIONAL NOTHING DAY

I like to be doing nothing to some purpose. That is what leisure means.
—Alan Bennett

In 1973, National Nothing Day was established "to provide Americans with one national day when they can just sit without celebrating, observing, or honoring anything." It's your kind of day.

Today I will take the challenge and fill my time with nothing at all.

January 17

LESS THAN PURE

I used to be Snow White . . . but I drifted.
–Mae West

We all were. We all did. That's life.

Today I will drift once more, with feeling.

January 18

CONSERVING ENERGY

Never teach a pig to sing. It wastes your time and annoys the pig.
–Author Unknown

If you want to be a good teacher, find a student who wants to learn. Good students make good teachers. Pigs are notoriously poor students.

Today I will only teach a pig something it really wants to know.

January 19

LOST IN SPACE

The Concorde is great. It gives you three extra hours to find your luggage.
–Bob Hope

The faster you move, the more often ordinary things disappear into the void. Your keys get lost, your luggage wanders off, you forget where you parked the car, your partner vanishes. Moving at warp speed messes up the natural rhythms of the universe, and your stuff routinely gets sucked into the cosmic vortices.

Today I'll slow down until I catch up with myself.

January 20

WHISTLING WHILE YOU WORK

If work were such a splendid thing,
the rich would have kept more of it for themselves.
–Bruce Grocott

Rich people tell you how good it is to work hard. Then they hire people to do their work for them. While their workers are working, they go out and play. That's nice work if you can get it.

Today I will be generous and share my work with others.

January 21

FOND FORGETFULNESS

I'm in the prime of senility.
    –Joel Chandler Harris

Y ou stand in the middle of the kitchen and wonder why you're there. You can't retrieve the right word until everyone's gone home. You forget to take the vitamins that improve memory. You make lists and lose them. Welcome to the onset of senility.

I can forget today.

January 22

KILLER WORK

It's true, hard work never killed anybody, but I figure why take the chance?
    –Ronald Reagan

T hey told you that hard work was good for you, that it would build your character. That was their story. They never told you that hard work could kill you. Happily, you can figure that out for yourself.

Today I'll refuse to let my work be the death of me.

January 23

OLD HABITS NEVER DIE

A dog teaches a boy fidelity, perseverance,
and to turn around three times before lying down.
—Robert Benchley

Some of your habits are as strange today as they were yesterday. You probably have no idea where you got them or why you still do them. And your endearing ways continue to amaze and confound those around you.

Today I will refrain from barking at the mail carrier.

January 24

GLITTERING ACCIDENTS

The meek shall inherit the earth, but not the mineral rights.
—John Paul Getty

While building Sutter's sawmill near Coloma, California, in 1848, James W. Marshall accidentally discovered gold. He was overjoyed and tried to keep it a secret but word got out and the gold rush was on. He had to share his find, his claim, his stash. He was no longer joyous.

Today I could strike gold and still be left in the dust.

January 25

FINISHING LAST

If at first you don't succeed, you're running about average.
                                        —M.H. Alderson

In a perfect world you would never have to struggle with failure. You would succeed the first time, every time. So would everyone else. The world just doesn't work that way. Welcome to the land of the less-than-perfect.

> If, at first, I don't succeed today, I'll try, try again;
> then I'll give up and go to the movies.

January 26

MISSING PERSONS

Be alone and make friends with your sanity.
                                        —Enid Howarth and Jan Tras

So you're all alone. You haven't been chosen for the football team, the school play, or the astronaut training program. Your dance card is empty. Your phone isn't ringing. Your mail's stopped coming. You're surrounded by silence. What a blessing!

> Today I will savor my solitude, revel in the emptiness of my day,
> and rejoice in my sanity.

January 27

ROSE-COLORED BIFOCALS

Happiness? That's nothing more than health and a poor memory.
—Albert Schweitzer

Your memory deceives you. Even the good old days had their bad old nights. If the past looks rosier than the present, the present will look even rosier in the future. Be grateful you have a memory, even if it is dented and distorted.

Today, if I'm at all healthy, I'll remember to be happy.

January 28

NATIONAL KAZOO DAY

One man's musical comedy is another man's soap opera.
—Enid Howarth and Jan Tras

This is the day to expand your imperfect musical abilities. Impress lovers of fine classical music by moving onward and upward from tissue paper and comb. You can be a fearless one-person band. You can toot your own kazoo.

Today I will be in tune wherever I go.

January 29

ONLY THE LONELY

Just remember, we're all in this alone.
—Lily Tomlin

You think you're the only one. You are. Look around. Everyone else is the only one, too. This is a group phenomenon. Our aloneness is our connection. Think about it, but not too much.

> Tonight I will take advantage of being alone
> and sleep diagonally across the bed.

January 30

KINKY DINING

I'm at the age where food has taken the place of sex in my life.
In fact, I've just had a mirror put over my kitchen table,
—Rodney Dangerfield

Invite your most delicious friends to kinky dinners. Indulge your peculiar appetites and weird tastes. Slow down and savor every morsel. Steam up the mirror.

> Today I will pack a lunch to remember.

January 31

Morning Mirror Blues

You've heard of the three ages of man: youth, age,
and "you're looking wonderful!"
—Francis Joseph, Cardinal Spellman

So today you look your age. You're counting grey hairs and laugh lines. Your wrinkles announce that you've been somewhere, that you know something, that you've lived a little, maybe a lot. Darling, you look wonderful!

Today I will be kind to the cranky old person within.

February 1

Slow Dancing

Health is merely the slowest possible rate at which one can die.
—Author Unknown

Even if you exercise every day, eat the purest foods, and take all your vitamins, one day you will die. It happens to the best of us and the worst of us. You can only influence the quality of your life between now and then.

Today I will influence the rate at which I'm dying.

February 2

GROUNDHOG DAY

Change is inevitable, except from a vending machine.
–Author Unknown

Change will happen whether you're ready or not. Without change, you'd be reliving Groundhog Day every day, stuck forever with your kindergarten teacher, your junior high zits, your first job, your first date. Change is your friend. It's your life.

Today I will accept all change, especially from vending machines.

February 3

RELATIONSHIP BLUES

Men and women, women and men. It will never work.
–Erica Jong

You thought that relationship thing would work. You gave it your all. Sometimes it clicks. Sometimes it doesn't. You're probably running about average.

Today I'll replace the "men and women, women and men" stuff
with something safe, like sky diving.

February 4

LIFE'S LITTLE SURPRISES

Life is what happens when you're making other plans.
—Betty Talmadge

Your meticulous plans are supposed to unfold just as you imagine they will. It's not supposed to rain on your party, your passion, or your parade. The universe's lack of cooperation is rude and totally unacceptable. Bad design.

Today life will be a mess despite all my longing
for tidiness and predictability.

February 5

PIT STOP

When you hit bottom and there's nothing but darkness,
keep your eye on the star shining over the pit.
—Enid Howarth and Jan Tras

The tiniest glimmer of optimism keeps fisherman fishing, runners running, teachers teaching, preachers preaching. When you're in the pits and it's really dark, look around. You're in good company. The best people fall into pits. It's as inevitable as being on top.

Today I will see my unhappiness as
just one more pit stop on the road of life.

February 6

THE BLAME GAME

For every action there is an equal and opposite criticism.
                                        –Author Unknown

Blaming is a universal sport. No matter what you do, no matter how well you do it, someone will be there to complain. You can run but you can't hide from criticism. It's everywhere. Don't take it personally.

Today someone somewhere will remind me that I am less than perfect.

February 7

THE MORNING AFTER

It is no time for mirth and laughter,
The cold, grey dawn of the morning after.
                                        –George Ade

Today is National Hangover Awareness Day. It commemorates some of the most memorable hangovers in history. It especially honors those who celebrate Babe Ruth's birthday (February 6) and survive the morning after. All participants must sponsor their own hangovers.

Today I will not test my body's ability
to bounce back from extreme partying.

February 8

LIVING WITH INJUSTICE

No good deed goes unpunished.
—Author Unknown

You always believed that if you were good and gave to people, they would be equally kind and giving to you. You longed for equity, reciprocity, and happy endings. Then you grew up.

> Today I will be an adult and pretend not to mind
> that the cosmos is unjust.

February 9

TELLING TALL TALES

I can handle rejection and abandonment, but only when I'm lying to myself.
—Enid Howarth

If you live long enough, you will be rejected, abandoned, and hurt by someone, someday. Some people will not love you or want to be with you and your delightful imperfections. Clearly, those people have limited imaginations, poor judgment, and terrible taste.

> Today, no matter what anyone says or does,
> I will not lie to or abandon my sweet and imperfect self.

February 10

FRIENDLY FITNESS

I think making love is the best form of exercise.
—Cary Grant

The cobwebs on your exercycle, your rowing machine, and your stair stepper are telling you something. Consider other forms of exercise. Throw a tantrum. Adopt a child. Run amuck. Swim the English Channel. Snowshoe to Alaska. Move a mountain. Make love.

Today I will include steamy, sweaty, and stimulating
as part of my daily exercise program.

February 11

DISTRACTED LISTENING

A good listener is usually thinking about something else.
—Kin Hubbard

It's easy to be fooled by silence, to believe that quiet people are thoughtful, insightful, and deep. If you imagine their silence means they're mesmerized by your every word, don't risk asking them to repeat what you just said.

Today I'll say something outrageous and see who's listening.

February 12

EMULATING ABE

My father taught me to work, but not to love it. I never did like to work, and I don't deny it. I'd rather read, tell stories, crack jokes, talk, laugh—anything but work.
—Abraham Lincoln

They told you that you weren't serious enough to be president. Not so. Even presidents get to be practical jokers, to tell tall tales, talk nonsense, and laugh at the state of the Union. Practice your stand-up comedy. You might get to play the White House.

Today I'll be the life of the party, just like Lincoln,
and wait for the nomination.

February 13

RUNNING AWAY

No problem is too big to run away from.
—Charles M. Schulz

You thought you had to turn and face your big problem. You don't. You can run and hide. Stay away as long as you can. Rest up. It'll be waiting for you when you return, and wonder where you've been.

Today I will run away from my big personal problems
and concentrate on something manageable, like world peace.

February 14

VALENTINE'S DAY

Roses are red
Violets are blue.
Your Valentine's funny
And so are you.

On this day of perfect schmaltz and romance, honor your beloved's bumps and lumps—and your own as well. Sing "My Funny Valentine" off key but full of heart.

Today I will let my chocolate heart melt as I remember
my funniest valentines.

February 15

FUSSING WITH FASHION

I base most of my fashion taste on what doesn't itch.
—Gilda Radner

If you choose comfort over style, you will be marching to a different designer. You will be out of step in the hard, cold, costly world of fashion. But fashion changes every twenty minutes, so you may be ahead of your time.

Today I will make my own fashion statements and start a trend.

February 16

AVOIDING ARROGANCE

Flattery is alright—if you don't inhale.
—Adlai E. Stevenson

Flattery is a great recreational drug. It goes right to your head. It's the smokey part of smoke and mirrors. Avoid getting hooked on it.

Today I will refuse to inhale and just say no to flattery.

February 17

HANDS-ON LEARNING

I hear and I forget. I see and I remember. I do and I understand.
—Chinese Proverb

Real understanding comes from doing. There is no substitute for experience. Think driving. Think cooking. Think parenting. Think sex.

Today I will move beyond thinking into the daring world of doing.

February 18

BRAVO FOR BOVINES

Laughing stock: cattle with a sense of humor.
—Author Unknown

On this day in 1930, Elm Farm Ollie, a fearless dairy cow, was the first bovine to fly and be milked in an airplane. She hailed from Missouri, but is now claimed by Wisconsin, the Dairy State, where folks remember her by singing the "Bovine Cantata" from Moocini's lyric opera, *Madame Butterfat.*

Today I will order a milkshake and toast life's littlest triumphs.

February 19

PASSIVE ACHIEVEMENT

Gomez' Law: If you don't throw it, they can't hit it.
—Lefty Gomez

If you don't answer the phone, they can't talk to you. If you don't argue, there's no one to fight with. If you don't compete, the game will be over. You don't have to play. You can take your toys and go home.

Today I will establish and maintain a policy of creative withdrawal.

February 20

FLAUNTING FAILURE

Failure has gone to his head.
—Wilson Mizner

Perhaps you are the perfect failure. You've failed at so many things for so many years and you've done it with such style and grace, you are the expert. You are the best—and six months later, no one even remembers.

Today I will teach others that failure can be its own reward.

February 21

LEAP BEFORE YOU LOOK

Mistrust first impulses: they are always good.
—Charles de Talleyrand

If you trust your first impulses and follow them, too many good things might happen. Too many old things might have to change. You might have to rev up your engine and fasten your seat belt. It could be a very bumpy ride.

Today I will let my first impulse have its way with me.

February 22

Odd Man Out

Be virtuous and you will be eccentric.
—Mark Twain

Your eccentricities keep you out of sync with the rest of the world, swimming upstream. Maybe you're just more virtuous than the average frog. Let any criticism roll off your lily pad. It isn't easy being green.

Today I will be perfectly virtuous and eccentric, warts and all.

February 23

Not Dead Yet

About the only good thing you can say
about old age is, it's better than being dead!
—Stephen Leacock

If you were perfectly in control, you would never grow old and die. You would never slow down. You would stay young, vigorous, fertile, and strong forever. You're not perfectly in control.

Today I'll be glad I'm not dead yet.

February 24

CHERRIES JUBILEE

Life is just a bowl of pits.
—Rodney Dangerfield

It's true. Inside every cherry there's a pit. Inside avocados, mangos, and peaches, too. Pits are everywhere—inconvenient, annoying, and dangerous. It's the pits.

Today I'll be grateful for the fruit that surrounds the pits.

February 25

DEAL ME IN

The game of life is not so much in holding a good hand
as in playing a poor hand well.
—H.T. Leslie

The big dealer in the sky hands out wild cards, marked cards, royal flushes, pairs of deuces, garbage. You don't get to shuffle or to deal; you only get to play. Like the song says, "You got to know when to hold 'em, know when to fold 'em, know when to walk away, know when to run."

Today I will ante up, hedge my bets, bluff as needed, and play to win.

February 26

DOG TRAINING

He has every attribute of a dog except loyalty.
—Senator Thomas P. Gore

He may have a cold nose, a shiny coat, a beautiful tail, and be willing to roll over and play dead for you. His ability to bark at strangers or fetch your slippers may not be enough, however, if he's disloyal. Some imperfections matter more than others.

Today I will give up trying to teach my old dog new tricks.

February 27

MENTAL MISCHIEF

Murder is always a mistake. One should never do anything
that one cannot talk about after dinner.
—Oscar Wilde

You can dream of committing mischief, mayhem, and murder. You can imagine being a troublemaker, a terrorist, a tyrant. Dreaming and imagining are better than going to jail, where the after-dinner conversation is less than perfect.

Today I will only make mistakes I can talk about after dinner.

February 28

EXCEEDINGLY EXCESSIVE

Too much of a good thing is simply wonderful.
—Liberace

Everything has gone your way. You've had your cake and eaten it, too. You've had far more than your share. Your life has been bountiful and abundant, sinful and decadent. You've been blessed. Guilt is not required.

Today I will allow my life to be too much of a good thing.

February 29

TIME TRICKS

Time is a circus, always packing up and moving away.
—Ben Hecht

Leap year happens because it takes an awkward 365.2422 days for the earth to orbit the sun. Since 46 B.C., February has been chosen to accommodate this complication by adding an extra day every four years. If it's so hard to balance the calendar, no wonder you're struggling with your checkbook.

Today I will leap over my urge to make everything come out even.

March 1

CREATING MONSTERS

Frankenstein and My Fair Lady *are really the same story.*
—William Holden

Designing people has unpredictable consequences. It's always better to create things that won't clobber you later. Ask Henry Higgins. Ask Dr. Frankenstein. Ask your parents.

Today I will resist my urge to play God.

March 2

NOT THE LONELIEST NUMBER

I was never less alone than while by myself.
—Edward Gibbon

The worst kind of loneliness is feeling totally alone while surrounded by other people. The best kind of loneliness is fishing.

Today I'll take myself fishing.

March 3

SPARKLING DEFECTS

Real diamonds have real flaws; only the fakes are perfect.
—Enid Howarth and Jan Tras

Zircons, rhinestones, faux pearls, silk flowers, rubber chickens, and plastic bananas are perfect and forever. You're not. You're a real diamond in the rough. Let your flaws sparkle in the sunshine, in the moonlight, in the dark.

Today I will dazzle the world with a flaw to remember.

March 4

TAKING A RAIN CHECK

I have never taken any exercise except sleeping and resting.
—Mark Twain

National Procrastination Week begins sometime today or tomorrow. It promotes the benefits of relaxing, delaying obligations, resisting progress, and refusing to be hurried. If you have been postponing your life, today is your kind of day.

Today I will put off doing my life for one more day.

March 5

SHOCKING SUCCESS

Behind every successful man stands a surprised mother-in-law.
—Hubert Humphrey

People are surprised by your success. Even you are surprised by your success. Success often happens to those who least expect or deserve it, including you.

Today I will send roses to someone who doubts me.

March 6

INDECISION REVISITED

When you come to a fork in the road, take it.
—Yogi Berra

All important decisions are based on insufficient information. So are all unimportant decisions. Choose one. If it's wrong, don't worry. There's always another fork ahead.

Today I'll make a decision and pretend to know what I'm doing.

March 7

CONSUMER REMORSE

A study of economics usually reveals that the best time to buy anything is last year.
—Marty Allen

Finding the bargain, the best deal, the wisest investment can drive any consumer crazy. You can spend all your time doing the research, the comparison shopping, the bargain hunting. Hindsight always knows what you should have bought yesterday.

Today I will forgive myself for being economically challenged.

March 8

OVER-EXPOSED

Never do card tricks for the group you play poker with.
—Author Unknown

It's much smarter and sexier to reveal just a little at a time. It keeps folks interested and leaves you with an ace or two up your sleeve. If you reveal everything, you'll never be able to bluff again.

Today I will be savvy about exposing my hand.

March 9

CRISIS MANAGEMENT

When God sneezed, I didn't know what to say.
                                                    –Henny Youngman

When God sneezes, you can't say, "God bless you." The last time God sneezed, the Rockies rose up out of the Great Plains and tidal waves rolled across the Pacific. There isn't a blessing big enough to cover this situation.

Today, I'll remind myself that even an imperfect blessing
is nothing to sneeze at.

March 10

RELATIVITY

When a man sits with a pretty girl for an hour, it seems like a minute.
But let him sit on a hot stove for a minute—and it's longer than any hour.
That's relativity.
                                                    –Albert Einstein

Time expands and contracts and knows nothing of clocks or watches. Some nights are far too long. Some evenings are far too short. Morning often comes too soon. Time can stand still or move at warp speed. It's not about seconds or minutes or hours. It's about you.

Today I will dance to the rhythms of my internal clock.

March 11

BORING OSCARS

The capacity of human beings to bore one another
seems to be vastly greater than that of any other animals.
−H.L. Mencken

If you're tired of spending $7 or more to be bored at the movies, take heart. On this day, Most Boring Film Awards will be given to the most tiresome films of the previous year. Categories include Comedy, Action, and Big Stars−Big Flops.

Today I will honor myself with a lifetime achievement award
for my finest flops.

March 12

HIDDEN CHARMS

Weed—a plant whose virtues have not yet been discovered.
−Ralph Waldo Emerson

Yesterday you were junk. Today you're a collectible. Yesterday you were Clark Kent. Today you're Superman. Yesterday you were bread mold. Today you're penicillin.

Today I will find a higher use for the lowly weed within.

March 13

Avoiding Labor Pains

The most popular labor-saving device is still money.
—Phyllis George

If you long for a faithful assistant, a servant, an army of robots to cater to your every whim and meet your every need, think again. Reducing your whims and needs might be your best labor-saving device.

Today I will curb my greed and work less.

March 14

Working Yourself to Death

All work and no play makes Jack a dull boy—and Jill a wealthy widow.
—Evan Esar

If you are a workaholic—frazzled, overachieving, and dull—keep your life insurance current. If you don't play with your beneficiaries now, they'll play later without you.

Today I will make time to play with the people I love.

March 15

Counting Blessings

Happiness is no creditor at the door and nobody sick.
–Chinese proverb

Happiness isn't about lots of good stuff. It's about no bad stuff. It's about being grateful for the absence of poverty and pain. You're probably already happy and don't even know it.

Today I will be happy that I am relatively healthy
and there are no wolves at the door.

March 16

Shooting from the Hip

He who hesitates is probably right.
—Author Unknown

There is some middle ground between being recklessly impulsive (Ready! Fire! Aim!) and being overly cautious (Ready! Aim! Aim! Aim!). Find the middle ground. Hesitate. Be thoughtful. You will be less likely to shoot yourself or anyone else in the foot.

Today I will adjust my sights and not go off half-cocked.

March 17

St. Patrick's Day

Where would the Irish be without someone to be Irish at?
—Elizabeth Bowen

Who says bigger is better? The world's shortest Saint Patrick's Day Parade, barely ninety-seven feet long, takes place in Maryville, Missouri. For less than half a block, floats and marchers wind down Buchanan Street for a few minutes. The parade route, painted green, is shortened every year.

Today I will celebrate with something very short and very green.

March 18

Pink Slips

Relationships are hard. It's like a full-time job, and we should treat it like one.
If your boyfriend or girlfriend wants to leave you, they should give you
two weeks' notice. There should be severance pay, and before they leave you,
they should have to find you a temp.
—Bob Ettinger

Relationships are temporary and don't come with any written guarantees. Any one of us can be laid off at any time. There is no long-term security.

Today I will design a golden parachute to cover relationship downsizing.

March 19

UNDERCOVER

Underneath this flabby exterior is an enormous lack of character.
—Oscar Levant

A less than perfect exterior is often a clue to someone's less than perfect interior. Sometimes a perfect exterior only tells you that someone has a very good personal trainer or plastic surgeon.

Today I will allow my imperfect inside to shine
through my imperfect outside.

March 20

SPRING FORWARD

He gave her a look you could have poured on a waffle.
—Ring Lardner

It's a spring thing. The sap is rising. The snap, crackle, and pop of hormones can be heard around the world. Everyone's dreaming sweet, syrupy, sappy dreams. Birds do it; bees do it; even educated fleas do it. You want to do it, too.

Today I unwrap my libido and let it thaw.

March 21

Alternative Medicine

I have a perfect cure for a sore throat—cut it.
—Alfred Hitchcock

When you're sick, put yourself out of your misery by any legal means. Hibernate, moan, beg, medicate. Be creative. If all else fails, go to the south of France, take the sea air, and expire in style.

Today I will pamper and indulge my sick and unhappy body.

March 22

Born to Trek

Space travel is an extravagant feat of technological exhibitionism.
—Lewis Mumford

Riverside, Iowa, where few men have gone before, has chosen itself as the future birthplace of James T. Kirk, captain of the Starship Enterprise. His birth will occur on this date in the year 2228. Prepare to party.

Today I will go forth and prosper.

March 23

EIGHTEEN FOREVER

Actually, I'm eighteen. I've just lived hard.
—Clint Eastwood

Maybe no one knows that on the inside you're really only eighteen. Maybe you just look as old as Paul Newman, Lauren Bacall, Sophia Loren, or Sean Connery. Time flies when you're having fun.

Today I will let the eighteen-year-old within take a well-deserved break.

March 24

LOVE'S SWEET SONG

Love doesn't make the world go 'round.
Love is what makes the ride worthwhile.
—Franklin P. Jones

With or without love, the world keeps on spinning. With love, it spins a little more smoothly, and it hums a sweeter song.

Today I will sing love songs to my imperfect life.

March 25

INVESTMENT BLUES

She's been dwindling in the stock market.
—Dr. Maxwell Kurtz

You haven't always invested as wisely as you might have. Sometimes there were no capital gains. Sometimes there were no gains at all. Sometimes there were only losses. It's nothing personal.

Today I will call my broker and weep. That's what I pay him for.

March 26

FAKING IT

Logic is the art of going wrong with confidence.
—Joseph Wood Krutch

Cover your ass with confidence. It works better than facts or reason. Confidence can get you to the top before anyone finds out that you're unreasonable and just plain scared.

Today, right or wrong, I will fake it 'til I make it.

March 27

INEPT MODELING

I learned an awful lot from him by doing the opposite.
—Howard Hawks on Cecil B. De Mille

Doing things your own way will make you an example for somebody, some-where. And somebody, somewhere, will insist on doing the very opposite. So much for being a perfect role model.

Today I will be an inadequate role model,
leaving others to sort out their own confusion.

March 28

STICKY LABELS

A narcissist is someone better-looking than you are.
—Gore Vidal

Anyone can stick positive and negative labels on exactly the same activity. You can call yourself "spontaneous," and label someone else "out of control." You per-severe; they're stubborn. You're committed; they're stuck. You love good things; they're self-indulgent. You're busy; they're hyperactive. You're relaxed; they're lazy. You take care of yourself; they're narcissists.

Today I'll notice who's doing the labeling.

March 29

THORNS AND ROSES

My grandfather always said that living is like licking honey off a thorn.
—Louis Adamic

Life is a dangerous sport. Play it carefully. It takes great skill, cunning, and agility to savor its sweetness without getting stuck or wounded.

Today I will enjoy life's honey and be prepared to bleed.

March 30

REPUTATION LOST AND FOUND

I'm the girl who lost her reputation and never missed it.
—Mae West

Once upon a time people cared about their reputations. They struggled to present a perfect image to the world. Some people didn't care, and they had much more fun.

Today I will gleefully add another skeleton to my closet.

April 1

April Fool's Day

The first of April, some do say,
Is set apart for All Fools' Day,
But why the people call it so,
Nor I nor they themselves do know.
— *Poor Robin's Almanack*, 1760

Today is your day. You have permission to be a prankster, to wear rings on your fingers and bells on your toes. You can't be wise until you're willing to be a fool.

Today I will play the fool with all my foolish friends.

April 2

Meetings for Fun and Profit

Meetings are indispensable when you don't want to do anything.
— John Kenneth Galbraith

Meetings are blessed interruptions. They meet everyone's need for sharing, small talk, and cat naps. They're a noble excuse to linger over coffee and snacks while getting paid. They're a time-honored substitute for real work.

Today I will value the hidden benefits and multiple perks of meetings.

April 3

FIGURING THE ODDS

When you go to the bullfight, don't bet on the bull.
—Author Unknown

You could play the lottery and get back forty cents for every dollar you spend—if you're lucky. You could go to the bullfight, ignore the odds, and keep betting on the bull. You and the bull will lose every time.

Today I will bet on the matador—the guy with the sequins,
the red cape, and the pointy sword.

April 4

WISE OLD BONES

When I feel like exercising, I just lie down until the feeling goes away.
—Robert M. Hutchins

Like the urge to diet, the temptation to exercise often needs to be resisted, thwarted, and denied. Do not allow your mind to make overzealous demands on your wise old bones. Listen to your body's rhythm and respect its longing to rest.

Today I will just lie down and rethink my push toward perfect fitness.

April 5

KILLER DIETS

One of the problems with diets is that the first three letters spell "die!"
—Barbara Johnson

Your unconscious thinks you're trying to kill yourself when you diet. That's why it keeps you hovering near the cookie counter, the deli department, the potato chip aisle. Your instinct for self-preservation will overcome your willpower every time. No wonder dieting feels like dying.

Today I will refuse to let dieting be the death of me.

April 6

CARVING YOUR EPITAPH

Many people's tombstones should read, "Died at 30. Buried at 60."
—Nicholas Murray Butler

This day is dedicated to the proposition that having a boring epitaph is a fate worse than death. Inspirational gravestones include: "Here lies W.C. Fields. I would rather be living in Philadelphia." Dorothy Parker suggested, "Excuse my dust." John Sparrow offered, "Without you, Heaven would be too dull to bear. / And Hell would not be Hell if you are there."

Today I will write a snappy epitaph for myself,
and plan to revise it on this date next year.

April 7

FREQUENT-FAILURE MILES

My life has been nothing but a failure.
–Claude Monet

Surely you have already been a failure. You've flunked a test, lost your keys, forgotten your phone number, spilled your drink, and dented a fender—at least once. Surely you've let someone down, stood someone up, broken a heart or two, lied. You have enough frequent-failure miles to take you anywhere.

Today I will gaze at Monet's waterlilies and contemplate failure.

April 8

CHICKEN LITTLE DAY

What happens if you get scared half to death twice?
–Author Unknown

This day commemorates fear and hysteria. It honors Chicken Little's efforts to convince Henny Penny, Turkey Lurkey, and Foxey Loxey that the sky really is falling. Awards are given to organizations or individuals "who have frightened the daylights out of large numbers of people" with scientifically dubious predictions of impending doom and disaster.

Today I will honor the chicken within.

April 9

THE CUTTING EDGE

If you must control something, control
something that won't resent you afterwards.
−Enid Howarth and Jan Tras

Do not bonsai your friends. Do not topiary your relatives. They will resent your efforts to shape them. If you must mold something, groom your closet, file your toenails, trim your philodendron. That will be enough for one day.

Today I will resist my wild urge to shape and control the people I love.

April 10

THE JOY OF SUFFERING

A man will renounce any pleasures you like but will not give up his suffering.
−George Gurdjieff

You could spend the next ten years suffering at home while your worst enemies are surfing in Hawaii. As they catch the next wave, you could be drowning in an ocean of pain. Your anguish won't keep anyone off the beach—except you.

Today I'll give up suffering no matter how much it hurts.

April 11

REARING CHILDREN

Children today are tyrants. They contradict their parents,
gobble their food, and tyrannize their teachers.
—Socrates

Since the beginning of time, children have been badly judged by their elders. They are not perfect, never have been, never will be. They are often stubborn, snotty, tyrannical, angry, and defiant. Just like you used to be.

Today I will be kind to all children and their less-than-perfect parents.

April 12

POTBELLIED

You can only hold your stomach in for so many years.
—Burt Reynolds

Face it, your body is changing as you read this. It's been changing since the day you were born. It's not going to stop now. You can pretend to be thinner and younger than you are. You're not.

Today I will loosen my belt, breathe deeply,
and enjoy the fullness of my reality.

April 13

APPROACHING THE PROMISED LAND

There must be a Shangri-la beyond the Himalayas of work.
—Enid Howarth and Jan Tras

Climbing the career ladder can be like climbing Mount Everest. You can't do it alone. You need the right equipment, the right friends, good weather, good lungs, and good luck. There's usually no time to smell the flowers. There are no flowers to smell.

Today I will rest on a rocky ledge and dream of Shangri-la.

April 14

KISSLESS

Smile: it's the second best thing you can do with your lips.
—Author Unknown

If you need kisses, kiss someone. If no one's around, try whistling: "Just put your lips together and blow." Or try chocolate. Chocolate isn't the same as a kiss, but it may be the best you can do today. And, as substitutes go, it's pretty darn good.

Today I'll embrace second best and smile.

April 15

Deep in the Heart of Taxes

What is the difference between a taxidermist and a tax collector?
The taxidermist takes only your skin.
—Mark Twain

In 1770, English chemist Joseph Priestly discovered that a small cube of latex could be used to rub out pencil marks. Instantly, mistakes were easier to make and to cover. You and your accountant owe him your everlasting gratitude.

Today I will send in my most imaginative tax return.

April 16

Hanging on to Happiness

. . . he who kisses the Joy as it flies,
Lives in Eternity's sunrise.
—William Blake

So, things are good today. You want to stop time and live in this golden moment forever. Unfortunately, joy flies. Happily, so does sorrow. You can't control or hold on to any of it. Change is inevitable; give it a kiss.

Today I will embrace my fleeting moment of happiness.

April 17

TARGET PRACTICE

*The fascination of shooting as a sport depends almost wholly
on whether you are at the right or wrong end of a gun.*
—P.G. Wodehouse

Demanding perfection seems totally reasonable when you hold the gun. It hardly ever seems reasonable when you're the target. It can be devastating when you're both the gunman and the target, aiming for absolute perfection from yourself. Position is everything in life.

Today I will take up a new sport and quit taking potshots at myself.

April 18

TRYING NO MORE

If only we'd stop trying to be happy, we could have a pretty good time.
—Edith Wharton

Under all your complaints, all your whining and moaning, you're already much happier than you think you are. You're already doing what works for you. You may not admit it, but you really are having a pretty good time most of the time.

Today I'll have a good time instead of trying to be happy.

April 19

BURNING BRIDGES

The hardest thing to learn in life is which bridge to cross and which to burn.
—David Russell

Some bridges lead to connection. Some bridges lead to disaster. Some bridges invite you to stand in the middle and watch the water flow downstream. No one ever tells you which is which. Extreme caution is advised.

Today I'll burn that bridge when I come to it.

April 20

UNDERVALUED SPORTS DAY

The only athletic sport I ever mastered was backgammon.
—Douglas Jerrold

Attention all sports fans. Today, in Beaver, Oklahoma, a highly specialized athletic event takes place: the World Cow Chip Throwing Championship. This competition draws dung flingers from around the world, including politicians and lawyers, who are known to be especially proficient and highly skilled at this sport.

Today I will fling it with the best of them.

April 21

AEROBIC DECISION-MAKING

A conclusion is the place where you got tired of thinking.
—Author Unknown

Think, think, think. You've sifted all the evidence, studied all the facts, listed the pros and cons. You're tired of the whole process, suffering from a paralysis of analysis. Go ahead and make a decision. Sleep on it. You can always change your mind in the morning.

Today, before I get tired of thinking, I will be reckless,
perch on the edge, take a leap of faith, and jump to a conclusion.

April 22

WHINE AND ROSES

Ah, love—the walks over soft grass, the smiles over candlelight,
the arguments over just about everything else.
—Max Headroom

Love is not only about perfect romance and living happily ever after. It's also about rainy days, mortgages, the flu, and disagreements about silly things like money, power, and sex. Expect this. Lovers are always a little less than perfect.

Today I will kiss and make up with my most beloved adversary.

April 23

Blazing Self-doubt

When in doubt, wear red.
—Bill Blass

Red puts color in your cheeks. It makes you appear bigger, bolder, braver. It's good for intimidation, the illusion of power, and a temporary energy surge. Use it.

Today I will just wear red.

April 24

Sinning

Between two evils, I always pick the one I've never tried before.
—Mae West

When in doubt, do something new and bad. Be adventurous. Boldly go to new depths and try not to hit bottom. Explore. Experiment. Get into trouble. Get out of it. Enjoy.

Today I will sin and err in ways I never imagined.

April 25

FINAL ERRORS

I hope I've made the last big mistake of my life.
—Dorothy Rogers

Mistakes come in sizes, shapes, and colors you can't even imagine. Bloopers you haven't even dreamed of are waiting for you. In time, even successes can turn out to be mistakes. Take heart. Being imperfect is forever.

Today I will expect to make at least one mistake, and it won't be my last.

April 26

THE COST OF MONEY

Being young is not having any money;
being young is not minding not having any money.
—Katharine Whitehorn

When you were young, you believed someone else would always pay the bills, bail you out, cover your debts. Then you got your own credit cards, your own phone, your own insurance, your own car payments. And you thought you could afford to be a grownup. . . .

Today I'll be an adult no matter how much it costs.

April 27

Bottoming Out

It's lonely at the bottom.
—Enid Howarth and Jan Tras

You've hit bottom and you're all alone. The truth is you'd be alone at the top. You'd be alone in the middle. It happens. Life is often an alone kind of thing.

I will call today's journal entry, "A View from the Bottom."

April 28

Sleeping In

It was such a lovely day I thought it a pity to get up.
—W. Somerset Maugham

You don't need a blizzard or the flu to stay in bed for a day. You don't need total burnout or a nervous breakdown to take a morning off. You only need the courage to lie there and let the day begin without you.

Today I will unplug my guilty conscience
and plan to spend a lovely day in bed.

59

April 29

SEX RIDES AGAIN

It's been so long since I made love I can't remember who gets tied up.
—Joan Rivers

It's been a while. Your recall is fading. Your libido's rusting. You no longer remember details, but your body maintains a fond memory or two. There are cherished moments and secrets that sustain you. You never forget how to ride a bicycle, either.

I'll spend today riding my bike
and watching the XXX-rated movies in my head.

April 30

DEATH BY TELEVISION

If a man watches three football games in a row,
he should be declared legally dead.
—Erma Bombeck

Sports fans like reclining in big easy chairs and watching other people run up and down a hundred yards of grass. Fans like seeing people bump, shove, kick, tackle, and get knocked over. All this violent physical activity can make any viewer tired, even comatose. Check for a pulse after a long silence on a Sunday afternoon.

Today I will encourage every TV addict in my family to make a living will.

May 1

CHUBBY

In my own mind I am still that fat brunette from Toledo.
–Gloria Steinem

Because your genes determine the shape and size of your jeans, the body you inherited will never look like the one you long for. Surrender to your imperfect DNA. Appreciate that you turned out as well as you did. You could be in much worse shape than you are right now.

Today I will be imperfect, fat, and happy.

May 2

BIRTHDAY COSTS

You know you're getting old when the candles cost more than the cake.
–Bob Hope

If you buy a bigger cake every year, you won't have this problem. The cake will always cost more than the candles. See to it. There are always creative solutions to the problems of aging.

Today I will put a down payment on a king-sized birthday cake.

May 3

SPARE CHANGE

Money is better than poverty, if only for financial reasons.
–Woody Allen

You may have been taught that being poor is a noble and worthy way to live your life. But being committed to poverty is as useless as being attached to wealth, and not nearly as much fun.

Today I will be financially unreasonable.

May 4

TEST ANXIETY

I think animal testing is a terrible idea;
they get all nervous and give the wrong answers.
–Author Unknown

You know how it feels to be tested: standing in front of your own internal firing squad, blindfolded and ready to be shot at dawn. Imperfect test takers are their own best executioners.

Today I will grade on the curve.

May 5

International Unmother's Day

Don't compromise yourself. You are all you've got.
—Janis Joplin

This day honors all women who are not mothers, those who cannot or choose not to have children. This day reminds us that a woman's worth, like a man's, is not based on being a parent or living up to conventional expectations. It celebrates variety, differences, courage, and individual choice.

Today I will celebrate the nonparent within.

May 6

Home Sweet Home

Maybe the Wizard of Oz was right: we're already home.
—Enid Howarth and Jan Tras

Maybe we already have the heart, the brains, and the courage that we thought we needed to find somewhere else. Maybe we don't need a wizard. Maybe there are no wizards. Maybe we're already home.

Today I will be at home no matter where I am.

May 7

CREATIVE NUTRITION

I like to think of banana cream pie as a fruit.
—"Pat Prints" calendar

Surely chocolate is a vegetable, one of the four basic food groups. Ice cream is a dairy product, an excellent source of calcium. Cookies are made from wheat—a carbohydrate and a great source of fiber. Sugar is a vital and necessary brain food.

Today I will use chocolate to balance my diet.

May 8

BLIND SPOTS

If the blind lead the blind, both shall fall into the ditch.
—Matthew 15:14

Even the most committed helpers have their blind spots. They stumble and bumble and have to feel their way, just like you do. Find a helper whose limitations are different from yours, so both of you can stay vertical more of the time.

I will spend today lying in the ditch, rethinking my blind spots.

May 9

BAD MOTHER'S DAY

Once I got past my anger toward my mother,
I began to excel in volleyball and modeling.
 —Gabrielle Reece

It's hard to believe, but your mother was young once, even younger than you are now. She was once a baby, a little girl, an adolescent. Then she became your mother. Go forth and play volleyball.

Today I will get past my childhood anger and work on my serve.

May 10

GOOFING UP

In the country of the blind, the one-eyed king can still goof up.
 —Laurence J. Peter

You will goof up today. You will spindle, fold, or mutilate something before tonight is over. Why should today be different from any other day?

Today I will goof up royally without even trying.

May 11

INVENTING INNOCENCE

I can remember Doris Day before she was a virgin.
—Groucho Marx

Once upon a time you, too, were virginal. You remember. Then you had an experience or two. You remember. You've been there, done that. It was probably less than perfect—like everything you remember.

Today I will wear white and honor the virgin within.

May 12

CHALLENGING AUTHORITY

It's always better to apologize afterwards than to ask permission.
—Author Unknown

You've known since you were twelve that if you ask, you're likely to hear "No." So don't ask. Just do it. You take the risk. You pay the price. You get the payoff. You cope with the consequences.

Today I will go for it and be prepared to grovel.

May 13

Hummingbird Goose Day

There is no place to go, and so we travel!
 −Edward Dahlberg

On this day, Coos Bay, Oregon, honors ride-sharing. Folks gather to watch the benevolent geese who allow tiny humming birds to hitch a ride and snuggle deep in their goose down as they migrate north. Today is a reminder that you don't always have to migrate alone. Honk if you love geese.

Today I will share the ride as I travel north on the highway of life.

May 14

Frightening Ideas

I can't understand why people are frightened of new ideas.
I'm frightened of the old ones.
 −John Cage

New ideas and old ideas are just ideas. They have no substance, no power, except the power you give them. But they can imprison your imagination and lock up your creativity for life. That's a sentence you don't deserve.

Today I will break out of an old idea
and try one that's new and frightening.

May 15

ODDBALL OUT

On some planets, I would be considered normal.
            —Enid Howarth and Jan Tras

Face it, you are not normal and never have been. You have weird thoughts, peculiar desires, quirky habits, and unspeakable dreams. On some undiscovered planet, there are others just like you living perfectly ordinary lives. But not here.

Today I will reach beyond this solar system to find my people.

May 16

WEAR PURPLE FOR PEACE DAY

Humankind cannot bear very much reality.
            —T.S. Eliot

Today is the very first intergalactic holiday. Everyone who longs to meet an extraterrestrial is expected to wear purple to welcome and demonstrate peaceful intentions toward visitors from other galaxies.

Today I will disguise myself as an eggplant
and put a welcome mat on my landing strip.

May 17

NATIONAL PICKLE WEEK BEGINS

Every man is a damn fool for at least five minutes every day;
wisdom consists of not exceeding the limit.
                                        −Elbert Hubbard

On this day, Atkins, Arkansas, home of the incredible, edible fried dill pickle, celebrates the world's most absurd vegetable with a pickle pageant and tours of pickle plants. It's a dilly of a day to get pickled.

Today I will crown myself Pickle of the Year, bumps and all.

May 18

FAIRNESS FLACK

The trouble with referees is that they just don't care which side wins.
                                        −Tom Canterbury

Referees are not cheerleaders. They get booed and cheered no matter what call they make. It's a dirty job, being neutral, fair, and following the rules.

Today I will remember that whatever call I make,
someone, somewhere, will hate me.

May 19

PURRSISTANCE

Cats seem to go on the principle that it never
does any harm to ask for what you want.
 —Joseph Wood Krutch

Cats know everything about persistence. They start with sleeping in your chair. Then they purr, rub against your legs, lie on your notebook, do stupid pet tricks, and complain until you pay attention. The squeaky cat gets the cream. There's something to learn from cats.

Today I will purrsist in asking for what I want.

May 20

PRAYER POWER

When the gods wish to punish us, they answer our prayers.
 —Oscar Wilde

You'd better hope that the gods have more vision and better sense than you do. Hopefully, they will monitor and censor your prayers and only answer the ones that are really good for you. Which may be the reason you haven't won the lottery.

Today I will pray for help, just in case my prayers are answered.

May 21

THE FRENCH HAVE A WORD FOR IT

A psychiatrist is a man who goes to the Folies-Bergère
and looks at the audience.
—Bishop Mervyn Stockwood

The Folies-Bergère is just like life. Each person sees a slightly different show. Some look at the costumes and sets. Some watch the dancing. Some see the sexy stuff. Some don't.

Today I will keep an eye out for whatever I've been missing.

May 22

SEX IS THE ANSWER

Sex is one of the nine reasons for reincarnation.
The other eight are unimportant.
—Henry Miller

If you've ever asked why you were born here on earth at this time and in this place, sex is the answer. If you've ever wondered what life is all about, sex is the answer. If you've ever wondered why there are past lives and future lives, sex is the answer. What was the question?

Today I will remember that sex is the simple answer
to every complex question.

May 23

CREATIVE ECONOMICS

I've been rich and I've been poor and rich is better.
—Sophie Tucker

Given the choice, take the money and run. Gamble in Monaco, fly to Paris, ride the Orient Express, wear sable. When the money runs out, do poverty with style and grace. Gamble at Monopoly, fly off the handle, ride your in-laws, wear plaid.

Today I'll use my beer pocketbook to indulge my champagne tastes.

May 24

BROOKLYN BRIDGE DAY

There's a sucker born every minute.
—P.T. Barnum

On this day in 1883, the Brooklyn Bridge was opened. The Bridge cost $16 million and took only fourteen years to construct. It has been sold over and over again. It is still for sale.

Today I will make a down payment on the Brooklyn Bridge
and honor the sucker within.

May 25

TIMELY REVENGE

Time wounds all heels.
—Jane Ace

If you wait long enough, the heel might be wounded, the villain might be boiled in oil, the bad guy might slip on the banana peel. If not in this life, surely in the next. But you may not live long enough to see it. Life doesn't run on your timetable, and it isn't fair.

Today I will place my longing for absolute justice in the hands of the gods.

May 26

AVOIDING SERIOUSNESS

Not a shred of evidence exists in favor of the idea that life is serious.
—Brendan Gill

Once upon a time they tried to teach you to be serious. They said schoolwork was more important than recess. They said you had to get good grades and follow the rules. They urged you to grow up, straighten out, settle down, and be like them. Misery loves company.

Today I will renew my commitment to recess and field trips.

May 27

FEEDING LONELINESS

It's lonely at the top, but you eat better.
—Author Unknown

Loneliness has nothing to do with being at the top. It's lonely at the bottom, too, where the food's really bad and the company's worse.

Today I may be lonely, but I won't go hungry.

May 28

INVITATION TO DISAPPOINTMENT

Nobody can let you down unless you set yourself up.
—Enid Howarth and Jan Tras

Setting yourself up for disappointment means wanting life to be different. It isn't. It means wanting people to be different. They aren't. You know this. You hate it. You forget it. You need to be reminded.

Today I will neither set myself up nor let myself down.

May 29

GENDER MADNESS

I have yet to hear a man ask for advice on
how to combine marriage and a career.
–Gloria Steinem

Once marriage was in the hands of women, and careers were in the hands of men. Now all our hands are full, being breadwinners and bread bakers, home buyers and homemakers, spouses and successes. No wonder everyone's stressed and confused.

Today I will advise the president how to combine marriage and a career.

May 30

FENDER BENDER AWARENESS DAY

There are two kinds of pedestrians—the quick and the dead.
–Author Unknown

Today is the anniversary of the first auto accident, the first ding heard round the world. In 1896, Henry Wells, driving a Duryea Motor Wagon, collided with a bicycle rider, Evylyn Thomas, in New York City, fender bender capital of the world. She survived. She was a New Yorker.

Today I will remember that to ding is human, to forgive, divine.

May 31

PLAYING THE ODDS

In a fight between you and the world, back the world.
—Frank Zappa

When you take on the world, be sure your life insurance is paid up, that you have a living will, that your family knows your last wishes. Ask yourself if you really want to be a sacrificial lamb.

Today I will refuse to end up as shish kebob.

June 1

NO ROAD MAP

Life can only be understood backwards; but it must be lived forwards.
—Soren Kierkegaard

Looking in your rearview mirror tells you where you've been, not where you're headed. You'll have about as much control over what's ahead as you had over what's behind. You never really know where the road will lead. You hardly understand where you've been. That's called adventure.

Today there is no road map for the state I'm in.

June 2

"First Woman Runs the House" Anniversary

A woman's place is in the House and in the Senate.
—Gloria Steinem

Today's history lesson: On this date in 1921, Ms. Alice Robertson of Oklahoma became the first woman to preside over the U.S. House of Representatives. She held this exalted position for half an hour and was never heard from again.

Today I will talk fast and bask in my thirty minutes of fame.

June 3

Mighty Casey's Strike-out

You can't think and hit at the same time.
—Yogi Berra

On June 3, 1888, "Casey at the Bat" was first published in the *San Francisco Examiner*. Ernest Thayer received $5 in payment for the poem and regarded the ballad's fame as a nuisance. His other writings are widely forgotten. Today, there is no joy in Mudville. Mighty Casey, the ultimate slugger, has struck out.

Today I will strike out with the best of them.

June 4

WORKING PAPERS

I love being a writer. What I can't stand is the paperwork.
                                            –Peter de Vries

You thought you'd found the ideal job at last. Then you began doing it. You found out it was tedious, mundane, and stressful as well as creative and stimulating. You couldn't have known all that until you were in the thick of it. There is no perfect job. That's why they call it work.

Today I'll remember why I took this job.

June 5

ORDINARY PEOPLE

Whatever you may be sure of, be sure of this—
that you are dreadfully like other people.
                                            –James Russell Lowell

No matter what your mother told you, you resemble other humans more than you resemble a Botticelli angel. You are as imperfect as most mortals and will never be more human than you are today.

Today I will be dreadfully like other people.

June 6

THE JOY OF FIGHTING

Never go to bed mad. Stay up and fight.
—Phyllis Diller

When times are hard, forget sleeping. Stay up and fight, then make up until morning. Creative conflict resolution can be the most fun.

Today I will make peace under the stars.

June 7

STDs

Life is a sexually transmitted disease.
—Guy Bellamy

So you thought the stork dropped you on the rooftop, that you were found under a cabbage leaf, that you were a gift from on high. In case you hadn't noticed, all those stories leave something out. Like sex.

Today, even if I can't believe it, I'll be thankful
that my parents had sex at least once.

June 8

OVERTURNING JEALOUSY

Jealousy is all the fun you think they had.
—Erica Jong

The script you're inventing about them is much racier than the script you're writing about yourself. No wonder their story seems so much wilder and steamier than your story. You're creating it.

Today I'll rewrite my story and make it much sexier than theirs.

June 9

GLAMOUR CHALLENGED

Any girl can be glamourous. All you have to do is stand still and look stupid.
—Hedy Lamarr

You know how to do that. You learned it from old Hollywood movies. You thought it was all about good looks, elegant clothes, and superior genes. Not so. It's about smoke, mirrors, and good editing.

Today I'll cultivate glamour and a vacant stare.

June 10

TICKLING GOD'S FUNNYBONE

If you want to make God laugh, tell Him/Her your plans.
–Author Unknown

You made foolproof picnic plans. You cast the *I Ching,* had your Tarot cards read, and your local astrologer did your chart. Everything was set and ready to go. You were reasonable, logical, and figured all the odds. It rained.

> Today I will acknowledge that my individual divinity
> has severe limitations.

June 11

BEDDING DOWN

I'm not the type who wants to go back to the land;
I am the type who wants to go back to the hotel.
–Fran Lebowitz

Know thyself. Whether you're low maintenance or high maintenance, into nature or into comfort, respect your own priorities. You've never been what the world thought you should be. Feel free to sell your camping gear.

> Today, instead of making dinner, I will make reservations.

June 12

LONELY AT THE TOP

Nobody roots for Goliath.
—Wilt Chamberlain

When you're a winner, some folks will feel left behind. Early warning signs of success may include envy, jealousy, and malicious gossip. Some folks won't be your fans, won't share your triumphs. Try being hugely successful. Notice who loves you anyway.

Today I will triumph and see who still wants to play with me.

June 13

GALLOPING INDECISION

I'm not confused, I'm just well-mixed.
—Robert Frost

You can see both sides of the issue. You can appreciate all the arguments. Every bit of evidence has some merit. There are pluses and minuses everywhere. You are well-balanced and well beyond decision-making.

Today I will admit that I am thoroughly confused.

June 14

Patient and Pushy

I am extraordinarily patient provided I get my own way in the end.
—Margaret Thatcher

Getting what you want right away is the most fun. Waiting is not so much fun. The least fun of all is waiting and not getting what you want. They taught you that patience was a virtue so you'd resist the urge to punch somebody out.

Today I will be extraordinarily patient and get my own way.

June 15

Wasted Youth

It is better to waste one's youth than to do nothing with it at all.
—Georges Courteline

When you were young, you did exactly what you had to do, and your misspent youth is now serving you well. You were bold, inventive, and resisted authority. That's what got you where you are today.

Today I will be kind to a young person
whose wasted youth is driving me crazy.

June 16

PARANOID ENVY

I envy paranoids; they actually feel people are paying attention to them.
−Susan Sontag

Maybe nobody's really concerned about your less than perfect complexion, body, manners, or performance. Maybe nobody's paying that much attention to you. Maybe you're the only one who's totally obsessed with your imperfections.

Today I'll let other people envy my paranoia.

June 17

SCANDALOUS

Happy is he who causes scandal.
−Salvador Dali

If you weren't afraid of causing scandal, you could be outrageous, wild, and shocking. If you spoke and lived your truth, you could, at last, be difficult, uproarious, and potentially very happy.

Today I will be scandalous and let the good times roll.

June 18

Luck of the Draw

Happiness is a temporary state of bliss that you don't deserve.
                                        −Enid Howarth and Jan Tras

Neither happiness nor sadness is about deserving. Bad guys get big rewards. Good guys get big trouble. Bad guys get rich. Good guys get struck by lightning. Before it's over, you'll get some misery you didn't earn. You'll get some undeserved happiness, too.

Today I will allow myself twenty whole minutes of undeserved bliss.

June 19

Progress Revisited

Progress was all right. Only it went on too long.
                                        −James Thurber

In some very civilized and progressive nations, people still enjoy leisurely afternoon meals, take naps, listen to music, dance, and spend time with their children. They move without haste, refuse to be stressed out, and the necessary work still gets done. That's real progress.

Today I will be a grain of sand in the whirling wheels of progress.

June 20

SUMMER SOLSTICE

Some are weather-wise, some are otherwise.
—Benjamin Franklin

The first day of summer is the longest day of the year and thus the shortest night of the year. In the Northern Hemisphere it's the beginning of summer. In the Southern Hemisphere it's the beginning of winter. It's an upside-down, right-side-up kind of day.

Today I will make hay while the sun shines.

June 21

WORKPLACE BLUES

I will only deceive and compromise myself in order to stay gainfully employed.
–Enid Howarth and Jan Tras

It's easier to be uncompromising and idealistic if you are independently wealthy. If you're a trust-fund baby, you know nothing about the struggle to keep body and soul together, food on the table, the check in the account, the wolves from the door. For most people, the only thing worse than working is not having a job.

Today I will honor my ability to deceive and
compromise myself as necessary.

June 22

ENOUGH ALREADY

I've got all the money I'll ever need . . . if I die by four o'clock.
                                                        −Henny Youngman

Try not to die by four o'clock. Stay alive and be poor if you have to. Financial security is an illusion. All security is an illusion. You'll figure it out.

Today I'll live with minimum security one hour at a time.

June 23

UNMANAGEABLE OLD FOLKS

Time and trouble will tame an advanced young woman,
but an advanced old woman is uncontrollable by any earthly force.
                                                        −Dorothy Sayers

If you thought that getting old meant slowing down, being placid, respectable, and boring, think again. Old people now call themselves grey panthers, climb mountains, and prowl in the moonlight. They are wild and out of control.

Today I will look forward to being old, vigorous, and very difficult.

June 24

WORLD-CLASS PROCRASTINATION

Never put off till tomorrow what you can do the day after tomorrow.
—Mark Twain

The most important tasks lose all urgency after three or four days. After a week they don't matter at all. After a month, they're merely a figment of your imagination. After a year, they've disappeared forever into the cosmic void.

Today I will put the world on hold.

June 25

CRYSTAL CLEAR CONFUSION

Mrs. Peter's Law:
Today, if you're not confused, you're just not thinking clearly.
—Irene Peter

The clearest thinkers know that everyone is confused. Some admit it, some muddle through, some fake it. Confusion can be the beginning of creativity. Lack of clarity can be a sign of higher intelligence.

Today I will embrace my confusion and pray that clarity will emerge.

June 26

Instant Success

Actually I'm an overnight success. But it took twenty years.
—Monty Hall

When you started down the road to overnight success, you didn't know it would take this long. Every successful person started as a beginner. You started as a beginner, too. In twenty years you will still be a beginner. Some things never change.

Today is the first day of my twenty-year plan
to become an overnight success.

June 27

Light before Dawn

Sometimes I've believed as many as six impossible things before breakfast.
—Lewis Carroll

When you consider only the possible, you diminish your brilliance, dampen your imagination, rain on your own inventiveness. It's easy to forget that your divine spark of creativity can light a fire even in a hurricane, even before breakfast.

Today I will pack my corn flakes and umbrella
and travel to worlds I haven't even invented yet.

June 28

THROUGH THE LOOKING GLASS

Seeing ourselves as others see us would probably
confirm our worst suspicions about them.
—Franklin P. Jones

People see what they want to see. They hear what they want to hear. They remember what they want to remember. And some of them still like you a lot. It's a miracle.

Today I will give thanks for all my short-sighted, hearing-impaired,
and forgetful friends.

June 29

JELLYROLL BLUES

It must be jelly, 'cause jam don't shake like that!
—Author Unknown

You may be built for comfort rather than speed, a soft and pillowy lover rather than a bag of bones. You may have been blessed with the luscious curves of a Reubens body, not the sharp angles of an El Greco. You may be living in the wrong century.

Today I will consider becoming a voluptuous nude model
for a life-drawing class.

June 30

COMPLEX SIMPLICITY

Live simply that others may simply live.
—Gandhi

Overindulged? Overburdened? Give everything away. Wear only a sheet. Walk by the sea with a begging bowl in your hand. If that seems impossible, find another solution that's somewhere between owning everything and owning nothing.

Today I will begin to simplify my life by giving one thing away.

July 1

A TAXING ANNIVERSARY

Capital punishment: The income tax.
—Jeff Hayes

On this date in 1862, President Abraham Lincoln levied the first income tax and made many accountants rich and happy. He also freed the slaves. Go figure.

Today I will not tax myself on any account.

July 2

HUMBLE PIE

Life is a long lesson in humility.
                    –James M. Barrie

Finding out that you're less than perfect is one of life's little surprises. It can be a shocking revelation, a humbling experience, or a devastating blow to the ego. It's one of the classic symptoms of growing up.

Today eating humble pie will be a piece of cake.

July 3

LOSING YOUR COOL

In saying what is obvious, never choose cunning. Yelling works better.
                    –Cynthia Ozick

You've said the obvious 432 times and no one listened. You've tried good manners, subtlety, and reason. Nothing worked. Now, try the element of surprise. Raise your voice. Jump up and down. Make a fuss. Create a ruckus. See what happens.

Today I will give up cunning and consider throwing a tantrum.

July 4

Rube Goldberg Day and Independence Day

Innovators have . . . always been derided as fools and madmen.
—Aldous Huxley

Rube Goldberg and the Declaration of Independence were born on this day. Thus, fireworks. Goldberg is famous for inventing the most elaborate and extraordinary machines to accomplish ordinary tasks. He would have combined a moon rocket, rickshaw, and steamship to travel from New York to New Jersey. He created the longest and most complicated processes—kind of like democracy.

Today I will invent the most convoluted ways to accomplish the simplest tasks.

July 5

Workaholics Day

Work is the curse of the drinking classes.
—Oscar Wilde

You can make some workaholics very happy by offering them the gift of your workload. Then you can go and party for them. They'll be too overextended to notice.

Today I will take a day off to honor Workaholics Day.

July 6

MAKING AN IMPRESSION

We made civilization in order to impress our girlfriends.
–Orson Welles

Now you know what drives men to compete in the Olympics, conquer Everest, rule nations, become giants of industry. Marc Antony was one of those guys. He fought and won to impress Cleopatra. The rest is history.

Today I will change the world and impress the hell out of somebody.

July 7

SHORT DIVISION

There are two kinds of people in this world: the kind who think there are two kinds of people, and the kind who know life just ain't that simple.
–Enid Howarth and Jan Tras

Sometimes the world seems divided into good guys and bad guys, friends and enemies, us and them, you and me, right and wrong, just fine and fatally flawed. If it were really that simple, we'd know who to love, who to hate, who to live with, who to live without. It's not, never was, never will be that simple.

Today I will add shades of grey
to my black-and-white model of the universe.

July 8

CLOTHESHORSE

I don't design clothes, I design dreams.
−Ralph Lauren

In designer jeans you can pretend to be a Texas rancher, a millionaire cowboy, a rodeo queen. You can imagine living the perfect rural life that never was—a life with no chores, no cares, no mortgages, no saddle sores, no mess, no mosquitoes, no manure.

Today I will put my bottom in a pair of dream jeans and ride, baby, ride.

July 9

TIMING IS EVERYTHING

Instant gratification takes too long.
−Carrie Fisher

If this were a perfect world, you'd never need to learn about delayed gratification. You'd get everything you wanted exactly when you wanted it. You'd have it all, and you'd have it right now. Alas, the big timetable in the sky wasn't designed with only you in mind.

Today I will cultivate patience
and quit trying to fast-forward the cosmic clock.

July 10

DESERVING EACH OTHER

You are imperfect and so is your significant other.
Any relationship that includes either of you will be imperfect.
–Enid Howarth and Jan Tras

If you had a perfect partner, you'd feel unworthy. If you were perfect, your partner would feel unworthy. Since both of you are imperfect, you are a sublime match. Stop complaining. You deserve each other.

Today I vow to live imperfectly ever after.

July 11

DIRTY WORDS DAY

Nobody, including the Supreme Court, knows what obscenity is.
–Norman Dorsen

Thomas Bowdler was born this day in England in 1754. He gave up his practice of medicine to cleanse the works of Shakespeare by removing what he considered to be improper and indecent words and expressions. Longing for purity, he cleaned up Gibbons' *Decline and Fall of the Roman Empire* and censored the X-rated Old Testament.

Today I will speak out and celebrate freedom of speech.

July 12

RISE AND WHINE

Middle age is when you still believe you'll feel better in the morning.
–Bob Hope

Once upon a time you did feel better in the morning. You were younger then. Now mornings are full of surprises. So is your body. So is your rate of recovery. Go easy on yourself.

I will move gently into this day.

July 13

THUMBS UP, THUMBS DOWN

Never judge a book by its movie.
–J.W. Eagan

Never judge movies by their hype. Never judge people by their looks. Never judge beginners by their mistakes. Never judge couples by only one spouse. Never judge parents by their children.

Today I will retire from judging and just enjoy the show.

July 14

GREAT EXPECTATIONS

Blessed is he who expects nothing, for he shall never be disappointed.
—Jonathan Swift

You want things to go your way. They won't always go your way. You want your expectations to get met. They won't always get met. You can either rethink your expectations or spend your life drowning in a pool of disappointment.

Today I will take the plunge and expect nothing.

July 15

BUTTERING UP

*Having the critics praise you is like having the hangman
say you've got a pretty neck.*
—Eli Wallach

Sometimes praise is nourishment. Sometimes it's poison. When praise comes your way, consider the source.

Today I won't let anyone butter me up for toast.

July 16

SAME OLD, SAME OLD

History repeats itself. That's one of the things wrong with history.
—Clarence Darrow

They said you would learn from experience. Not always true. They said you'd be smarter when you got older. Not always true. If you're still making the same mistakes over and over again, don't stop now. You're finally at the top of your learning curve.

Today I will admire my capacity for repetition, repetition, repetition.

July 17

WRONG WAY, CORRIGAN

Mind Like a Steel Trap—Rusty and Illegal in 37 States.
—Author Unknown

On this day in 1938, Douglas Corrigan left Brooklyn, New York, for Los Angeles, California, in a monoplane. He landed, twenty-eight hours and thirteen minutes later, in Dublin, Ireland, having followed the wrong end of the compass needle. Oops. Wrong way, Corrigan.

Today I will allow my unpredictable sense of direction
to take me for a joy ride.

July 18

YARD ENVY

If the grass is greener in the other fellow's yard,
let him worry about cutting it.

—Fred Allen

The less lawn you have, the less you have to mow and manicure. Having less can save you time, money, work, and worry. Less is more, and you've got plenty of less.

Today I will not covet my neighbor's grass.

July 19

OVERRATING WORK

Work is the refuge of people who have nothing better to do.

—Oscar Wilde

Once upon a time you chose to work. Now you're really good at it. It's easy to forget that there are other ways to spend time. Remember, there was life before work. There is life after work. There could even be life during work.

Today I will work a little, play a little,
and dream of having nothing better to do.

July 20

Better Late Than Never

If I had to live my life again, I'd make all the same mistakes—only sooner.
—Tallulah Bankhead

It may already be too late to make certain mistakes. Too bad. You missed your window of opportunity. You should have started sooner. Promise yourself to make every possible blunder at least once before you die.

Today I will make enough mistakes to make up
for the times when I did everything right.

July 21

Embracing Cowardice

"I'm very brave generally," he went on in a low voice,
"only today I happen to have a headache."
—Lewis Carroll

There are a million excuses, and they're all wonderful—from the most banal to the most preposterous. You can find the perfect excuse to avoid any challenge, any sign of growth or change. Excuses are your loyal friends and allies.

Today I will celebrate avoidance.

July 22

PAY THE PIPER DAY

*My parents finally realize that I'm kidnapped, and they snap
into action immediately: They rent out my room.*
—Woody Allen

Legend has it that, on this day in 1376, the German town of Hamlin hired a pied piper to lead their rats out of town. Unexpectedly, he succeeded. The town refused to pay him for his services. He took revenge by playing his pipe and luring all the children out of town, never to be seen again.

Today I will pay the exterminator bill.

July 23

BEING THERE

I've been things and seen places.
—Mae West

If you live long enough and let yourself live, you will be many things and see many places. You will be shocked, delighted, and amazed. You will live many lives and make many mistakes. Enjoy them all.

Today I'll go somewhere and watch someone happen.

July 24

PROFOUNDLY SHALLOW

Only the shallow know themselves.
—Oscar Wilde

Not knowing yourself at all may be a sign that you are deep and complex. Or it may be a sign that you've been splashing around in the shallow end of life's pool, playing videogames and watching soap operas.

Today, I will wade into deeper water and try not to drown.

July 25

FEAR OF FUN

Puritanism: The haunting fear that someone, somewhere may be happy.
—Author Unknown

So, you're worried that other people are having too much fun—laughing in the sunshine, cavorting on the slopes. They are. You could be one of them. Then other people could worry about you.

Today I will conquer my fear of unbridled happiness
and be recklessly joyful.

July 26

GREEN AND GRUMPY

I am not a vegetarian because I love animals;
I am a vegetarian because I hate plants.
–A. Whitney Brown

Do not let anyone cheerful near you today. Go to the nearest salad bar. Snarl at spinach. Complain at carrots. Pout at parsnips. Rage at radishes. Have a nice day.

Today I will be a cranky vegetarian.

July 27

WALK YOUR HOUSEPLANT DAY

Perennials are the ones that grow like weeds, biennials are the ones that die this year instead of next, and hardy annuals are the ones that never come up at all.
–Katharine Whitehorn

If you've already killed many house plants, take the survivors for a well-deserved walk. Talk to them. Acquaint them with their environment. As you stroll through the neighborhood, let them learn from other shrubs and trees how to survive despite imperfect care, neglect, and abuse.

Today I will honor my greenish thumb.

July 28

TERRY FOX DAY

The saints are the sinners who keep on going.
−Robert Louis Stevenson

Terry Fox was born on this day. Although cancer required the amputation of his right leg at age 18, he determined to devote the rest of his life to fighting the disease. He ran a "marathon of hope" across Canada in 1980, using an artificial leg. He ran from April to September, covering 3,328 miles and raising $24 million for cancer research.

Today I will rethink my limitations.

July 29

SWEET VENGEANCE

It's far easier to forgive an enemy after you've gotten even with him.
−Olin Miller

Plan your perfect revenge. Plot. Scheme. Choose your accomplices. Savor doing the dastardly deed. Appreciate your creativity and inventiveness. Don't do it. Take a hot bath instead. Let fate even the score.

Today I will drown my spite in a scented bubble bath.

July 30

Names to Remember

Forgive your enemies, but never forget their names.
                                                    –John F. Kennedy

Be smart. Keep your distance from folks who have harmed you. History tends to repeat itself. Back off and leave plenty of time and space for their improvement. They, like you, will always be entirely imperfect.

Today I will update my best enemy list.

July 31

Suffering One Day at a Time

If you suffer . . . it is a sure sign that you are alive.
                                                    –Elbert Hubbard

Welcome to a day of suffering. You wanted a bowl of cherries; today, life is the pits. You wanted a bed of roses; today, you get only thorns. If you're alive, some days are like that.

Suffering is such hard work I will only do it one day at a time.

August 1

CELEBRATING ANYTHING

I once wanted to become an atheist, but I gave up—they have no holidays.
—Henny Youngman

You need all the holidays you can get. Observe all birthdays, anniversaries, solstices, full moons, paydays, rain days, Wednesdays. Celebrate any and every non-event. Make fiestas, have parades, wear costumes, take the day off, live it up.

Today I will invent a holiday, hire a band, and party, party, party.

August 2

AMAZING GRACE

To live is so startling it leaves little time for anything else.
—Emily Dickinson

If you really open your eyes and look around, you will be amazed that there's so much splendor in the grass, so much sparkle in the tarmac, so many diamonds in the rough. Life is so dazzling, people are so miraculous, and the planet is so gorgeous that it's hard to go to work in the morning.

I will spend today being amazed and dazzled.

August 3

EAST MEETS WEST

In fourteen hundred and ninety-two,
Columbus sailed the ocean blue.
–Author Unknown

Columbus left Spain on this date in search of a shorter, more economical route to India. Aiming for the fabled treasures of the East, he ended up beached in the Bahamas, having discovered a surprisingly long route to India.

Today I will take the long way around,
allowing for navigational surprises and brave new worlds.

August 4

CONSENTING ADULTS

No one can make you feel inferior without your consent.
–Eleanor Roosevelt

No one can judge you until they've slogged a mile in your tennis shoes. You are less than perfect. So are your critics. So are your tennis shoes.

Today I will just say no to feeling inferior.

August 5

HUNTING AND GATHERING

For sale: parachute. Only used once, never opened, small stain.
–Author Unknown

Today celebrates the beginning of National Bargain Hunting Week. Especially designed for all hunters and gatherers, this week glorifies the fabulous flea market, the gigantic garage sale, the blockbuster bargain. It spotlights those tireless and courageous sellers and shoppers who transform trash into treasure.

Today I will join in the thrill of the hunt
and be prepared to make room for the bargain of a lifetime.

August 6

VERTICALLY CHALLENGED

Did you know that Gary Cooper was only 5'5"?
–Paul Williams

You don't have to be tall to be a romantic leading man. You can be a big star even if you're small. Think of Michael J. Fox, Mel Brooks, Buddy Hackett, Dudley Moore, Napoleon. Maybe you're one of them.

No matter what, I won't try out for the NBA today.

August 7

THEATER OF THE ABSURD

The Rich aren't like us—they pay less taxes.
—Peter de Vries

Rich people's dramas are different from yours. They have different plots, a different cast of characters, different costumes, and a different audience. The yacht needs repair; the stock market crashes; the limo driver is drinking; the bank balance is off by a million or so; the upstairs maid is sleeping with you-know-who.

Today I'll be thankful that my dramas are small scale and low budget.

August 8

UNNAMED AND UNAPPRECIATED

The day will come when everyone will be famous for fifteen minutes.
—Andy Warhol

Today is the birthday of the unsung African-American hero, Matthew A. Henson. Henson was Admiral Robert E. Peary's valet and fellow explorer. Unrecognized and unacknowledged, he and two unnamed Eskimos were really the first to reach the North Pole in 1909. Peary, the great white captain of the expedition, arrived minutes later to verify the location and take all the credit.

Today I will have a party for an unsung hero.

August 9

Factual Faux Pas

He's a real nowhere man, living in a nowhere land . . .
—The Beatles

It's said that Breckenridge, Colorado, was mistakenly left off the map in several historic treaties. On paper, it just didn't exist. On this day, Breckenridge celebrates its exclusion from America and revels in being a nowhere land.

Today I will exclude myself from ordinary reality.

August 10

Traffic Jam

Americans will put up with anything provided it doesn't block traffic.
—Dan Rather

If you're planning to throw a tantrum, cause trouble, change the world, just don't slow the flow. As long as traffic keeps moving, you can get away with almost anything.

Today I will avoid being a speed bump on the highway of life.

August 11

Boring Bedfellows

Somebody's boring me. . . . I think it's me.
                                   −Dylan Thomas

Notice how uninteresting, dull, and tiresome everyone is today. Blame them for your boredom. Urge them to be more entertaining. Complain that they're not stimulating enough. This will keep you from being bored.

I will spend today being a contented bore.

August 12

Punctuality and Punishment

The trouble with being punctual is that nobody's there to appreciate it.
                                   −Franklin P. Jones

You set your watch ten minutes ahead, set your alarm twenty minutes early, and arrived just in time to unlock the door, make the coffee, and wait for everyone else to show up. You've finally committed to being on time, and you're all by yourself—again.

Today I will be punctual and proud of it.

August 13

LEFT-HANDED DAY

When I'm not in my right mind, my left mind gets pretty crowded.
–Author Unknown

International Left Handers Day recognizes the frustrations of being left-handed in a right-handed world. This day celebrates the courage and imagination of left-handers, the folks who first learned how to do everything backwards.

Today I will be kind to a southpaw in a northpaw kind of world.

August 14

MIND OVER MATTER

Age is strictly a case of mind over matter.
If you don't mind, it doesn't matter.
–Jack Benny

They say you're only as old as you feel. Not true. You're probably older than you feel, older than you look, older than you say you are. You just won't admit it. Why should you?

Today I will deny reality and lie about my age.

August 15

PRACTICING MODERATION

I smoke in moderation, only one cigar at a time.
—Mark Twain

"To quit or not to quit," that's usually the question. If you went cold turkey and it didn't work, try moderation. Maybe your psyche can only handle one deprivation at a time.

Today I will only abuse myself in moderation.

August 16

CREATIVE SCHEDULING

For the happiest life, days should be rigorously planned,
nights left open to chance.
—Mignon McLaughlin

There's a reason your daily planner doesn't have spaces to schedule evening hours or nighttime appointments. If you must, rigorously plan and control your days. Let your nights just happen. Leave room for dreams.

I will release this night from my sweaty, controlling grasp
and let the good times roll.

August 17

RASH REVENGE

A good way to threaten somebody is to light a stick of dynamite,
then you call the guy and hold the burning fuse up to the phone.
"Hear that?" you say. "That's dynamite, baby."
–Author Unknown

You're feeling like the Incredible Hulk. You're determined, self-righteous, and pumped. But before you light that stick of dynamite, you'd better see who's holding it.

Today I will light no fuse before its time.

August 18

BREAKING OUT

I can't mate in captivity.
–Gloria Steinem

Living in captivity cramps your style, saps your vital fluids, weakens your primal urges, and inflames your temper. This response to feeling trapped may be industrialized society's covert method of population control.

Today I will shake the bars of my cage, plot my escape, and mate.

August 19

GRASS IS GREENER

*Happiness is an imaginary condition, formerly often
attributed by the living to the dead, now usually attributed
by adults to children, and by children to adults.*
—Thomas Szasz

Happiness always looks greener in someone else's front yard. They never seem to have crabgrass or weeds. They're never invaded by garden pests. From their side of the fence, your life looks enviable and perfectly green, too.

Today I will make peace with the crabgrass within.

August 20

TAKING A STAND

This wallpaper is killing me; one of us has to go.
—Oscar Wilde

So you've hated the carpet for twenty years and you're finally taking a stand. Your ultimatum lets you feel invincible for one glorious moment. Me or the carpet. My way or the highway. In a perfect world, they would always choose you. This is not a perfect world.

Today I will not paint myself into a corner.

August 21

Butting Out

Make someone happy today. Mind your own business.
–Author Unknown

Give others the gift of your silence. Allow them the pleasure of resolving their own issues. Spare them your brilliant advice and insightful solutions. Tend to your own affairs. Focus on your own life. Watch what happens.

Today I will sit back quietly as the world turns.

August 22

Hate Attack

I never hated a man enough to give him his diamonds back.
–Zsa Zsa Gabor

In the middle of a hate attack, make no irrevocable decisions. Do nothing to jeopardize your bank balance or your future. Get your priorities straight. Diamonds are a girl's best friend. Don't let hatred make you stupid.

Today I will hate less and sparkle plenty.

August 23

GREAT AMERICAN QUACKERS

If 50 million people say a foolish thing, it is still a foolish thing.
—Anatole France

Deming, New Mexico, hosts the world's greatest duck race on this date. It's the Kentucky Derby for well-trained, web-footed waddlers. The foolish festivities include the Crowning of the Duck Queen, Darling Duckling Contests, Best Dressed Duck, Tortilla Toss, and other daffy doings. This is not just an ordinary kind of day.

Today I will be as quackers as anyone in New Mexico.

August 24

LEISURELY CORRUPTION

Leisure tends to corrupt, and absolute leisure corrupts absolutely.
—Edgar A. Shoaff

You are an unproductive couch potato, lazy and decadent, languid and degenerate. They say you have no moral fiber. They may be right.

Today I will be cheerfully corrupted by too much leisure.

August 25

FRETTING

Don't worry. Be happy.
—Bobby McFerrin

Worry if it makes you happy. There are worse ways to spend time. If it doesn't make you happy, stop it. There are better ways to spend time. When you can't do anything else, worrying feels like doing something. It does do something. It darkens your day, slows your metabolism, dampens your mood, and scares you. It's a tough job, but someone has to do it.

Today I will be a happy worrier.

August 26

HEARING VOICES

It is astonishing how articulate one can become
when alone and raving at a radio.
—Stephen Fry

No one believed in the sounds that seemed to come from nowhere. Lee DeForest, born on this date in 1873, frightened and amazed the world with his radical invention—the wireless radio. He was accused of fraud and arrested for having made it possible for the first soap operas, newscasts, and commercials to be heard around the world.

Today I will tune in to voices that come from places I don't really understand.

August 27

BEING SOMEBODY

All my life, I always wanted to be somebody.
Now I see that I should have been more specific.
—Jane Wagner

You wanted to be the best—a contender, a star, a hero, a champion, a winner. You tried. You failed. Being more specific wouldn't have helped a bit.

Today I will remember that my nonspecific, generic,
undefined self is somebody, no matter what anybody says.

August 28

AMATEUR PARENTING

Parenthood remains the greatest single preserve of the amateur.
—Alvin Toffler

Amateurs do what they do for love, not for money. You were raised by amateurs. Your parents were less than perfect. So were your grandparents. So are you. But then again, so are the pros.

Today I will celebrate my amateur status
and raise my children the way I longed to be raised.

August 29

READY. SET. FAIL.

Two wrongs are only the beginning.
–Author Unknown

Beginnings are always hard. You're bound to make mistakes. It's nothing personal. You will fall down before you learn to walk. You will swallow a lot of water before you learn to swim. You will kiss a lot of frogs before you find royalty.

Today I will view every mistake as a slimy opportunity.

August 30

LONGING NO MORE

The good life starts only when you've stopped wanting a better one.
–Bertrand Russell

If your life is half full, it's also half empty. If you leave it half empty, you'll have more time to rest, sleep, and dream. You'll have time to realize that half full is enough, and perhaps more than enough. Maybe you're already swimming in grace and just haven't noticed.

Today I'll take stock and be satisfied with my surplus inventory.

August 31

THE PARENT TRAP

If you've never been hated by your child, you've never been a parent.
—Bette Davis

On the days when your interests conflict with the interests of your children, they will hate you and let you know it. Don't take it personally. All kids know how to hurt their parents. They have a gene for it. They have your gene for it.

Today I will remember how much I hated and loved my own parents.

September 1

NATIONAL IMPERFECTION MONTH

Perfection itself is imperfection.
—Vladimir Horowitz

Now is the time for all good perfectionists to come out of their closets and revel in their fabulous flaws and glorious imperfections. This Great American Celebration highlights losing things, falling down, asking for help, screwing up royally, laughing at ourselves, and reading chapters and verses from *The Joy of Imperfection.*

Today, and for the rest of this month,
I will celebrate being perfectly imperfect.

September 2

RUNNING LATE

Punctuality is the virtue of the bored.
                                    —Evelyn Waugh

People who always arrive on time are not like you. They are programmed to be prompt and perfect. Their clocks are designed to run faster than yours. They are aliens.

Today I will be a fashionably late earthling.

September 3

DIRTY SEX

Is sex dirty? Only if it's done right.
                                    —Woody Allen

Clean sex is like sex education in high school. All that theory and anatomy were no fun at all. Later, you found out that the classroom bears little or no relationship to real life. Any delightful human experience will be messier, more engaging, and less predictable than any flow chart or lesson plan.

Today I will study only unruly and untidy passions.

September 4

TECHNOLOGICALLY CHALLENGED

To err is human, but to really foul things up requires a computer.
                                                    −Author Unknown

You can only foul up your own little corner of the world. Computers can foul up the whole enchilada. And they don't apologize. They just do their thing, making gigantic goofs, creating mass confusion, and relentlessly taking over the planet.

Today I will only make people-sized mistakes.

September 5

FOOD LOVERS

Eat only what you love. Love what you eat.
                                    −Enid Howarth and Jan Tras

Don't waste a single calorie on any food that isn't delightful, delectable, and delicious. If it isn't real, if it doesn't make you tingle all over, don't eat it. Grown-ups are not required to clean their plates.

Today I will be the fussy eater I was born to be.

September 6

MONDAY BLUES

Monday is an awful way to spend 1/7th of your life.
                                        –Author Unknown

The work week is badly designed. Mondays happen before their time. Fridays never arrive soon enough. Weekends are always too short. Before you know it, it's Monday again.

Today I will find a way to make friends with Monday.

September 7

A FLAW TO REMEMBER

Never tell a story because it is true; tell it because it is a good story.
                                        –John Pentland Mahaffy

Today celebrates the opening of the New York Post Office Building. The motto over the door, "Neither snow, nor rain, nor heat, nor gloom of night, stays these couriers from the swift completion of their appointed rounds," is not an official motto. The Post Office has no motto. Today honors all mottoes and inscriptions that belong to no one.

Today I will move slowly toward the swift completion
of my appointed rounds, even if I have no rounds.

September 8

ECO-PASSION

They made love as though they were an endangered species.
                                    −Peter De Vries

Passion is more than just a tropical fruit. It's hot, it's sweaty, it's fun, it's trouble. It makes the world go around. It makes the world stop. We can pretend it doesn't matter. It does.

I am an endangered species and today I will act accordingly.

September 9

BELOVED MISTAKES

Experience is that marvelous thing that enables you
to recognize a mistake when you make it again.
                                    −Franklin P. Jones

You know mistakes when you meet them on the road. You even know their names and addresses. That's one of the advantages of being old and experienced. If you've lived long enough, you've met them all—probably more than once.

Today I will take an old mistake to lunch.

September 10

PIECE OF MIND

All happiness is in the mind.
                                            –H.G. Bohn

Where else would happiness be? All unhappiness is in the mind, too. You can tell yourself any story, give it any spin, make it tragic or comic, invent catastrophes, or devise happy endings. Unhappiness and happiness are both in the mind of the beholder.

Today I'll give myself a piece of my mind—the happy piece.

September 11

SELF-PRESERVATION

If I knew I would live this long, I'd have taken better care of myself.
                                            –Satchel Paige

It's shocking that you are as old as you are today. It's more shocking to imagine how old you'll be in ten or twenty years even if you take very good care of yourself. It's most shocking to imagine how old you'll be if you don't take care of yourself at all.

Today I'll exercise only the muscles I expect
to need and floss only the teeth I want to keep.

September 12

CREATIVE HOUSEKEEPING

Dust is a protective coating for fine furniture.
—Mario Buatta

Dust never hurt anything. Don't disturb it. It eliminates glare. You can write messages in it. Dust bunnies, growing and multiplying under the bed, may be weaving themselves into a rug while you sleep. Make friends with them.

Today I will surrender to dust.

September 13

GRIDLOCK INSPIRATION

Creative minds always have been known to survive any kind of bad training.
—Anna Freud

On this date in 1814, Francis Scott Key's ship was delayed in Baltimore harbor by the dastardly British attack on Fort Henry. The sails of his ship drooping, he had no choice but to watch the battle, which inspired him to pen the verses that, coupled with the tune of a popular drinking song, became our national anthem. Warriors and drinkers are America's heroes.

Today I will seek divine inspiration while stuck in traffic.

September 14

BUGGED FOR LIFE

*I love being married. It's so great to find that one special person
you want to annoy for the rest of your life.*
—Rita Rudner

It's not easy to find a special person to put up with you and your imperfections. It's not easy to put up with someone else's imperfections. It's easy to be annoyed with each other for years and years. That's what real commitment is all about.

Today I will invite my most annoying self to tea.

September 15

HAUNTED BY THE PAST

The past just came up and kicked me.
—Vanessa Williams

Like it or not, you're still closely related to the person you used to be. Your foolish choices, your misguided judgments, your big and small mistakes have made you who you are. You were imperfect then. You are imperfect now. You will continue to be imperfect.

Today I will be a living monument to my less-than-perfect past.

September 16

SWEET STRESS REDUCTION

Stressed, *spelled backwards, is* desserts.
—Loretta LaRoche

Some people live life backwards. They think they need to finish their okra before they can have lemon meringue pie. But those who know that life is short eat desserts first.

Today I'll melt my stress in a hot fudge sundae
before facing the carrots and broccoli.

September 17

COWBOY SERENITY

Rodeoing is about the only sport you can't fix. You'd have to talk to the bulls and the horses, and they wouldn't understand you.
—Bill Linderman

Life is about learning where you have leverage and where it's all bull. It's about when to get back in the saddle, when to keep your boots on the ground, and the wisdom to know the difference.

Today I will accept what I can fix, what has to stay broken,
and what speaks another language.

September 18

LOST IN SPACE

Of all the things I've lost, I miss my mind the most.
—Author Unknown

In Washington, D.C., on this date in 1793, George Washington laid the Capitol Building's cornerstone. That historic ceremony was the first and last time the stone, with its engraved silver plate, was ever seen. It was mysteriously lost, misplaced, or stolen, and to this date has never been found—just like those house keys you continue to wonder about.

Today I'll quit searching for long-lost cornerstones.

September 19

DUTY-FREE HAPPINESS

There's no duty we so much underrate as the duty of being happy.
—Robert Louis Stevenson

You are not obligated to be depressed, distressed, or miserable. You are not required to be depleted, sad, or sorry for yourself. If you took charge of your own happiness, you could sweeten your day, lighten your load, and amaze everyone who knows you. Try it. You can always go back to gloom and doom.

Today I will replace my need to be melancholy
with my obligation to be happy.

September 20

CALCULATING PERFECTION

Two imperfects don't make a perfect.
—Jan Tras

You and your partner are imperfect, no matter what anyone says. You know it; your partner knows it. Your relationship isn't perfect either, no matter what anyone thinks. There are no perfect relationships except in musical comedies and cyberspace.

Today I will quit tinkering with imperfections—mine, yours, and ours.

September 21

CHANGING COLOR

Fall is my favorite season in Los Angeles,
watching the birds change color and fall from the trees.
—David Letterman

Summer is over. It's time to end vacations, start school, rake leaves, put up storm windows, rev up the furnace. Ignore smog, global warming, and toxic fumes. Live in denial as long as you can. Spring is just around the corner.

Today I will fall in with the season.

September 22

VITAL SIGNS

Don't look forward to the day you stop suffering,
because when it comes you'll know you're dead.
—Tennessee Williams

In this life, suffering is required. It comes with the territory. Get used to it. A day without suffering is a vacation from ordinary reality, a day to remember, a small miracle. Since you're not dead yet, today probably won't be one of those days.

Today I will suffer a little—as little as possible.

September 23

BASEBALL'S BIGGEST BLUNDER

Man is Nature's sole mistake!
—W.S. Gilbert

On this date in 1908, during the decisive National League Pennant game between the Chicago Cubs and the New York Giants, the Giants had two men on base in the bottom of the 9th. When the batter hit a single to center field, Fred Merkle, the Giant runner on first, saw the winning run score and dashed happily to the dugout instead of advancing to second. The Cubs' second baseman tried to get the ball to tag Merkle out, but was stopped by fans streaming on to the field. The controversial game had to be replayed, and this time the Cubs won the pennant.

Today I'll remember to touch all bases before I go home.

September 24

GREAT ESCAPES

Art is the only way to run away without leaving home.
—Twyla Tharp

Overworked? Underpaid? Fed up? Tired of the folks you live with? Planning to drop out? Disappear? Ride off into the sunset? You could, but they'd probably find you anyway. It's easy to run, hard to stay away, impossible to hide.

Today I will run away, have an art attack,
and be home in time for dinner.

September 25

RESETTING YOUR CLOCK

If they try to rush me, I always say, "I've got one other speed—and it's slower."
—Glenn Ford

From the beginning you were told to hurry up, get a move on, finish up. You may never have heard, "Take all the time you need," "There's no hurry," "I'll wait for you." Now you're old enough to listen to your own internal clock, learn at your own rate, move at your own pace, even if it's snail slow.

Today I'll move like the tortoise and let the hares be harried.

September 26

FAT IS YOUR FRIEND

The leading cause of death among fashion models
is falling through street grates.
–Dave Barry

Carrying a few extra pounds has its advantages. It keeps you from being blown over by strong winds, from freezing in winter, from being mistaken for a lamppost. Extra weight provides padding, insulation, and some protection from the slings and arrows of outrageous fortune.

Today I'm happy to be a vulnerable stick figure
snug inside my cozy layer of cellulite.

September 27

NOTHING BUT THE FACTS

Don't talk unless you can improve the silence.
–Laurence C. Coughlin

The Warren Commission, on this date in 1964, issued its definitive report claiming that Lee Harvey Oswald acted alone in the assassination of President John F. Kennedy. Congress reopened the investigation in 1979 and issued its definitive report claiming that a conspiracy was most likely involved. In 1991, Oliver Stone made a definitive docudrama about the Kennedy assassination, telling yet another story. Stay tuned for updates.

Today I will expect all definitive explanations to be revised.

September 28

HEREDITY'S REVENGE

Levinson's 2nd Law: Insanity is hereditary—you can get it from your children.
                                                        –Sam Levinson

You can get other things from your children, too, like chicken pox, the new math, computer skills, forgotten knock-knock jokes, mystifying toys, fresh perspectives, and an amazing capacity for wonder. Heredity is a two-way street.

Today I will let my children teach me something new.

September 29

DEFEATING DEPRESSION

When women are depressed, they either eat or go shopping.
Men invade another country.
                                                        –Elayne Boosler

Basic tactical manual for gender-neutral depression: Plunder the refrigerator. Arm yourself with credit cards. Invade the mall. Attack the racks. Pillage the candy counter. Conquer your hunger.

Today I'll make cake, not war.

September 30

BAD POETRY DAY

My favorite poem is the one that starts, "Thirty days hath September"
because it actually tells you something.
—Groucho Marx

Today is your day to write a bad poem, or two, or five. Compose riotous rhymes, laughable limericks, sentimental sonnets, loony lyrics. Have an author's tea, a literary bash, a poetry reading. Give a prize for the worst verse of all.

Today I will give poetic license to the shy poet within.

October 1

NATIONAL CONTRADICTION MONTH

Food is an important part of a balanced diet.
—Fran Lebowitz

This month has been designated National Dental Hygiene Month as well as National Dessert Month. It's National Pork Month as well as Vegetarian Awareness Month. It's Hunger Awareness Month as well as National Pasta Month and National Pizza Month. It's a-little-something-for-everyone-to-chew-on month.

Today I will relish life's delicious little contradictions.

October 2

OLDER IS BETTER

Growing old isn't so bad when you consider the alternative.
—Maurice Chevalier

If you don't die first, you will get old. Don't fret. Old age can allow you to be free and difficult until the end. You can't always be in the springtime of your life. Autumn happens. So does winter. Relax into your own mortality.

Today I'll swing with the seasons.

October 3

DANGEROUS BEDFELLOWS

The lion and the calf shall lie down together, but the calf won't get much sleep.
—Woody Allen

Your sleep and your safety depend on who shares your den. Don't share your bed with lions or tigers or bears. It's probably best to stick with vegetarians and stay at the top of the food chain.

Tonight I will only lie down with creatures who snuggle
and nibble but never bite.

October 4

RESCHEDULING

The habitually punctual make all their mistakes right on time.
—Laurence J. Peter

In 1582, Pope Gregory XIII issued a bulletin which decreed that the day following Tuesday, October 4th, should be Friday, October 15th. He was correcting the Julian Calendar, which was, distressingly, ten days out of date. In 1582, hardly anyone noticed.

Today I will be one with the old Julian Calendar and happily out of date.

October 5

DISASTER PREPAREDNESS

Archie doesn't know how to worry without getting upset.
—Edith Bunker

Worry is always about the future. Lightning might strike. Bombs might drop. The world might come to an end. Then again, lightning might not strike, bombs might not drop, the world might not end.

Today I will let somone else worry about impending doom.

October 6

DIFFERENT DRUMMERS

All the things I really like to do are either illegal, immoral, or fattening.
—Alexander Woollcott

Anything you really like to do is, at this moment, being judged as bad for you. Enjoy your own sweet, misguided, and deviant choices. Your critics will never really understand you anyway.

Today I'll dance to my own conga drum
no matter who complains about the noise.

October 7

BAD IS BETTER

When I'm good, I'm very, very good, but when I'm bad, I'm better.
—Mae West

They told you that being good was good and being bad was bad. They lied.

Today I will get really good at being bad.

October 8

HUFFING AND PUFFING

The word aerobics *comes from two Greek words:* aero, *meaning "ability to,"*
and bics, *meaning "withstand tremendous boredom."*
—Dave Barry

Aerobic exercise was invented by people who have far greater tolerance for repetition and monotony than you do. If your heart needs pumping, you can find more delightful, imaginative, and personally satisfying ways to breathe hard, sweat, and increase muscle tone.

Today I will find a workout partner for some intense huffing and puffing.

October 9

SNOOZING FOR SUCCESS

Consciousness: that annoying time between naps.
—Author Unknown

Consciousness can be very tiring. If you've been awake, aware, sensitive, and alert today, you're probably exhausted. You deserve a rest.

Today I will nap between short bouts of consciousness.

October 10

RESIGNED

The buck stops here.
—Harry S. Truman

Vice President Spiro T. Agnew pleaded "no contest" to a charge of income tax evasion on this date in 1973. He became the second person ever to resign the office of vice president of the United States. Agnew served under President Richard M. Nixon. Busted.

Today I will be grateful that my income tax return
is not the lead story on the six o'clock news.

October 11

HEALTHY DYING

Health nuts are going to feel stupid someday,
lying in hospitals dying of nothing.
—Redd Foxx

Forget personal immortality. No matter how healthy you are, someday you're going to die of something. If you die from something medicine can't explain, they'll invent a term for whatever killed you, and your name might live forever.

Today I will give up being the healthiest nut who ever died.

October 12

FICTITIOUS FACTS

Get your facts first, and then you can distort them as much as you please.
—Mark Twain

Piet de Stuini, little-known Dutch sailor and spin doctor, convinced Christopher Columbus to falsify the date of his first landing in the New World. The ship's log claims that the discovery happened on October 12. The real date, October 13, might have scared off superstitious sailors, adventurers, and investors.

Today I will rewrite my own history,
bending the truth for fun and profit.

October 13

HIP HYPOCRISY

The secret of success is sincerity. Once you can fake that, you've got it made.
—Author Unknown

You, too, can learn to fake sincerity. You can even turn hypocrisy into a recipe for success. All it takes is a pound of smiles, a cup of dishonesty, a level teaspoon of chutzpah, and a pinch of villainy.

Today I will only cook up authentic sincerity
and let success simmer on the back burner.

October 14

OVERBOOKED

There can't be a crisis next week. My schedule is already full.
—Henry Kissinger

Busy, busy, busy. Nothing unexpected is allowed to happen. You have no flexibility, no time to have a toothache, a flat tire, or an orgasm. You've left no room in your life for minor catastrophes or major delights.

Today I will schedule in a tiny amount of dangerously free time.

October 15

OUTGROWING THE SILENT TREATMENT

No one ever called me pretty when I was a little girl.
—Marilyn Monroe

Maybe you were once as pretty as Marilyn and no one ever noticed or said anything. Maybe you weren't. At this very moment some people love how you look and some don't. They're probably still not saying anything, and they probably never will.

Today I will put a photo of my fabulous self on a calendar
and remember *Some Like It Hot.*

October 16

A Wilde and Crazy Day

Some cause happiness wherever they go, others whenever they go.
—Oscar Wilde

The great Irish poet, playwright and wit, Oscar Wilde, was born on this date in 1854. He wrote *The Picture of Dorian Gray, The Importance of Being Earnest,* and other acclaimed stories and plays. At the height of his career, he was jailed for two years on a morals charge. His dying words were said to have been, "This wallpaper is killing me; one of us has got to go."

Today I will cause a little happiness coming and going.

October 17

Tarnished Silver

Poor George, he can't help it—he was born with a silver foot in his mouth.
—Ann Richards on George Bush

It doesn't matter whether you were born into silver spoon wealth or wooden spoon poverty. You can still be a great embarrassment to your nearest and dearest every time you open your mouth. Your imperfections are your gift to them.

Today I will marvel at my amazing agility
as I continue to open mouth, insert foot.

October 18

HISTORICAL OVERSIGHT

Women are repeatedly accused of taking things personally.
I cannot see any other honest way of taking them.
—Marya Mannes

Once upon a time, Canadian law insisted that its women were less than people. But the course of history changed in 1929. Five feisty Canadian females, demanding equal rights for women, brought suit against their government. They won, on this date, for the first time, the right of all Canadian women to be recognized as persons.

Today I will treat myself as a real person, whatever sex I am.

October 19

SNEAKING A PEEK

You can observe a lot just by watching.
—Yogi Berra

If you can't see the forest for the trees, get out of the woods. If you're lost in the fog, leave the coast and move to higher ground. Try the long view instead of the close-up. New perspectives can lead to new insights, dizziness, and vertigo.

Today I will sneak a peek at my life and watch what I observe.

October 20

SMALL CHANGE

People change and forget to tell each other.
—Lillian Hellman

People change their minds. They change their hearts. They change their phone numbers, their last names, their partners, their noses, and their intentions. They don't tell you. You don't tell them, either. No wonder everybody's dancing in the dark.

Today I will change and notify someone.

October 21

SHORT-TERM THINKING

Six minutes of thinking of any kind is bound to lead to confusion and unhappiness.
—James Thurber

Your brain will not be available today. You won't be thoughtful, rational, or profound. Don't even try. If you want to succeed today, do something that doesn't require any thought. Watch clouds, smell flowers, listen to birds, sit still.

I will not waste this day trying to figure anything out.

October 22

CREEPING SENILITY

I never know how much of what I say is true.
–Bette Midler

It's hard to remember what you said twenty minutes ago, let alone what you said twenty days ago. Yesterday's truth is often today's fiction and tomorrow's prize-winning short story. Old age, time, and change make doubters of us all.

I am a work in progress, and my truths need constant revision.

October 23

BORE NO MORE

Never fear being vulgar, just boring.
–Diana Vreeland

If you weren't so afraid, think how much fun you could have. You could cause scandals, create havoc, be shocking, and shake up your little corner of the world. Vulgar and fearless people are willing to look bad, be foolish, and take risks. They are never boring.

Today I will practice being fearless and just a little bit vulgar.

October 24

THE NEW MATH

The secret of success is to keep the five guys who hate you away
from the five guys who haven't made up their minds.
—Casey Stengel

Notice who's on your team, who's against you, and who's undecided. Only play with people who love you. Outwit, out hit, and outrun anyone who doesn't. Keep score.

Today I will divide and conquer.

October 25

WEATHERING EXCUSES

I did a picture in England one winter, and it was so cold I almost got married.
—Shelley Winters

Weather is more important than most people realize. You can use it as an excuse for any decision. Blame the weather for moods, marriage, divorce, lust, depression, and cold feet. "The weather made me do it" is the ideal defense.

Today I will blame global warming for my imperfect life.

October 26

GRAND ILLUSIONS

Everything's changed except the way we think.
—Albert Einstein

Even when your beliefs don't work anymore, it's hard to let them go. They can remain fixed no matter what you've seen, learned, or experienced. Fixed ideas offer the grand illusion of safety and permanence in an ever-changing and dangerous world.

Today I'll bend before I break.

October 27

WALKING YOUR PET GORILLA

If you're planning to move through the world totally trusting and vulnerable, be sure you take your pet gorilla with you.
—Enid Howarth and Jan Tras

Trusting the world can be a dangerous sport. Not everyone plays the game by your rules. In the East they say, "Trust Allah and tie up your camel." The universe is full of surprises, and not all of them are pleasant.

Today I will trust more
and continue to work toward my black belt in karate.

October 28

BLIND AMBITION

By working faithfully eight hours a day, you may eventually
get to be a boss and work twelve hours a day.
—Robert Frost

Getting further up the ladder of success can mean more money, more perks, more power. It can also mean additional responsibility, harder decisions, extra paperwork, longer meetings, more stress, and higher taxes. Be careful what you wish for.

Today I'll reconsider my irrational urge to be the boss.

October 29

PERILOUS PREDICTIONS

You can only predict things after they have happened.
—Eugene Ionesco

In 1929, President Herbert Hoover declared, "The fundamental business of the country . . . is on a sound and prosperous basis." Four days later, on this date, the New York Stock Exchange crashed. Prices plummeted and the economy virtually collapsed. Billions of dollars were lost, and the nation was plunged into the Great Depression for the next ten years. So much for presidential predictions.

Today I will only predict things that have already happened.

October 30

WAR AND PEACE

You are your own best enemy.
—Enid Howarth and Jan Tras

You beat yourself up, judge yourself, shame, humiliate, and degrade yourself with great skill and agility. You've been practicing forever, and you do it every time. No other enemy can defeat you with more style and cunning than you can defeat yourself. You win. You lose.

Today I will make peace with my most formidable enemy—myself.

October 31

HALLOWEEN

Trick or treat,
Smell my feet,
Give me something good to eat.
—Author Unknown

Since the middle ages, All Hallows Eve has been associated with thoughts of the dead, spirits, and ghosts. Harry Houdini, world famous magician and escape artist, died on this date. He promised that his spirit would communicate with his wife from the other side. It didn't.

Today I will beware of goblins, ghosts, and rash promises.

November 1

DNA Blues

The problem with the gene pool is that there is no lifeguard.
—Author Unknown

Nothing can save you from your genes. Since your conception, they've been silently running your life, keeping you afloat. There is no other pool. Learn to swim.

Today I will trust my chromosomes to keep me from drowning.

November 2

Strange Bedfellows

My choice early in life was either to be a piano player in a whorehouse or a politician. And to tell the truth, there's hardly any difference.
—Harry S. Truman

Some jobs have fancier names and bigger salaries than others, but the oldest professions have more in common than you'd think. They require self-confidence, a sense of humor, the gift of gab, and the commitment to serve and entertain the public.

Today I will enjoy the absurdity of my job description.

November 3

FUTURE SHOCK

Of late I appear
To have reached that stage
When people look old
Who are only my age.
—Richard Armour

You were so busy living your life, you didn't even notice when everything started changing. Now that old person across the street is the same age you are. Now that old person in the shop window is you. It's shocking and entirely out of your hands.

Today I am older than I was yesterday. Tomorrow I will be even older.

November 4

HEARING VOICES

When we talk to God, we're praying. When God talks to us, we're schizophrenic.
—Lily Tomlin

If you're hearing voices inside your head, listen carefully. You may be getting inside information. Don't tell anyone. Remember what happened to Joan of Arc.

I will spend today in silence, talking and listening only to myself.

November 5

SURVIVAL NEED

I personally think we developed language because of our deep need to complain.
—Lily Tomlin

Complaining is an unrecognized basic human survival need. The mortality rate of noncomplainers is shockingly high. To live long and prosper, you must complain frequently, with wit, style, and grace. When life is perfect, you can stop complaining.

Today I will honor my genetic right to complain.

November 6

WAIST NOT, WANT NOT

You can never be too rich or too thin.
—Author Unknown

You can make yourself terminally ill fattening your wallet and slimming your waistline. You can kill yourself trying to perfect your body or your bank account. Don't bother. There will always be others who have more and weigh less than you do.

Today I will untie my self-esteem from
my purse strings and my tape measure.

November 7

THE FLIP SIDE

If you don't die first, you will get old.
—Enid Howarth and Jan Tras

It is shocking when doctors, policemen, politicians, and bosses are suddenly younger than you are. One day they, too, will have grey hair and laugh lines. So will you, if you're really lucky. It's better than the only other option.

Today I will age gracefully, kicking and screaming all the way.

November 8

BLACK HOLES

When it is dark enough, you can see the stars.
—Ralph Waldo Emerson

If you've tripped and fallen into a black hole, stay put. Don't move. All important decisions will wait until tomorrow. Defer. Rest. Look at the stars. Gain perspective. Soon, none of this will matter.

I will spend today in the dark and learn to navigate by the stars.

November 9

ORAL FIXATIONS

Smoking is very bad for you and should only be done because it looks so good. People who don't smoke have a terrible time finding something polite to do with their lips.
—P.J. O'Rourke

Busy lips are happy lips. Whistling is good. Talking is good. Singing is good. Smiling is good. Puckering is best.

Today I will put my two lips together, pucker up, and blow.

November 10

KNOW THYSELF

Trying to define yourself is like trying to bite your own teeth.
—Alan Watts

You're not the best person to figure out who you are. You've been with yourself too long. You have no perspective, no judgment, no objectivity, no distance. You need help. Ask people who know you.

Today I'll admit that I have no clue to my true identity.

November 11

LOSING THE WAR

Nobody will ever win the battle of the sexes.
There's just too much fraternizing with the enemy.
–Henry Kissinger

Maybe the other sex isn't really the enemy after all. Maybe they're only different from you. Maybe women really are from Venus and men from Mars. Maybe you could give up the struggle and settle for planetary truce. Then you could spend Sunday morning in bed with your former enemy.

Today I'll make love, not war.

November 12

FOLLOWING CLUES

Never go to a doctor whose office plants have died.
–Erma Bombeck

Useful information and clues are everywhere. Some are obvious. The writing is on the wall in big, bold letters. Don't ignore it. That dead philodendron could be you.

Today I'll play doctor and resuscitate my houseplants.

November 13

BUDDING HAPPINESS

If you would be happy for a day, cook a pot of rice.
If you would be happy for a week, buy a bottle of wine.
If you would be happy for a month, kill a pig.
If you would be happy for a year, get married.
If you would be happy for the rest of your life, be a gardener.
—Old Chinese proverb

Happiness is elusive and short-lived, but dirt is free and forever. There will always be dirt to dig in, to throw around, to cultivate, to roll in. Find some. Be happy.

Today I will search for happiness in a flowerpot.

November 14

FALLING BEHIND

Procrastination—the art of keeping up with yesterday.
—Don Marquis

You have created brilliant delaying tactics. Your excellent excuses, divine postponements, and stalling strategies are an unappreciated art form. Your genius for deferment has gone unrecognized too long.

Today I will accept last year's Nobel Prize for procrastination.

November 15

COLD HARD FACTS

The colder the X-ray table, the more of your body is required on it.
                                                    –Author Unknown

Once upon a time, when you were very young, someone taught you that life should be fair. They lied. It isn't. Sometimes it's hard and cold. Sometimes, suffering is required.

> Today I will ward off life's little chills by carrying
> my old reliable flannel blankie wherever I go.

November 16

REALITY TESTING

If three people tell you you're drunk, maybe you ought to lie down.
                                                    –Author Unknown

If you've been ignoring everyone's advice, listen up. They may be telling you something you need to know, something you've been resisting, something you hate to hear about yourself. Take the unthinkable to heart, then lie down and consider your options.

> Today I will suspend my disbelief and lie down.

November 17

Universal Gratitude

I want to thank everybody who made this day necessary.
—Yogi Berra

Be thankful you didn't make this day necessary. The earth turned and the sun rose without your input, your opinion, or your consent.

Today I will be thankful that I'm not responsible
for the workings of the universe.

November 18

Selective Attention

The art of being wise is the art of knowing what to overlook.
—William James

It's hard to overlook other people's flaws when you have a keen and critical eye. Wise and tactful people have figured out when to cultivate silence, when to look the other way, when to turn a deaf ear, when to speak, when to shut up.

Today I will be artful and overlook as much as possible.

November 19

IMMORTAL NO MORE

I don't want to achieve immortality through my work,
I want to achieve it through not dying.
—Woody Allen

If you work hard, you will die. If you don't work hard, you will die anyway. Do not kill yourself in pursuit of immortality.

Today I will leave my immortality in the hands of the gods.

November 20

PICK AND SHOVEL

Keeping house is as unpleasant and filthy as coal mining,
and the pay's a lot worse.
—P.J. O'Rourke

Today is National Clean Out Your Refrigerator Day. Without guilt, you can now toss out yesterday's pasta, last week's mystery meat, and the cottage cheese container with the furry green edges.

Today I will reconsider my career in mining.

November 21

GUT-WRENCHING INSIGHT

The pen is mightier than the sword!
The case for prescriptions rather than surgery.
—Marvin Kitman

U.S. Army surgeon William Beaumont was born on this date. He is famous for his research into digestion. An abdominal wound received by Canadian fur trapper Alexis St. Martin allowed the doctor to observe, for the first time, internal digestive processes. As St. Martin recovered, Beaumont tried to keep him around for further study, but St. Martin fled back to Canada and outlived his doctor by twenty years.

Today I will trust my gut.

November 22

SENSATIONAL READING

I never travel without my diary. One should always
have something sensational to read in the train.
—Oscar Wilde

You can transform your life into the steamy novel it was meant to be. Invent it. Write it. Be the fearless hero, the heartless villain, the sultry seducer, the champion of truth and justice. Make yourself laugh; make yourself cry. Be outrageous. Invite Hollywood to clamor for the movie rights.

Today I will begin writing my own uncensored autobiography
and never be bored again.

November 23

SIGHT GAGS

We are all here for a spell; get all the good laughs you can.
                                                    –Will Rogers

Say nothing but "Honk, Honk" today, in honor of Harpo Marx's birthday. Harpo was one of four brothers who made up the famous Marx brothers comedy team. Harpo wore a blonde curly wig and pretended to be mute, "speaking" with only a clown horn. He was an accomplished harpist, but he was so funny that nobody noticed.

Today I'll say nothing and toot my own horn.

November 24

PENNY WISE AND POUND FOOLISH

When a fellow says, "It ain't the money but the principle of the thing," it's the money.
                                                    –Frank McKinney Hubbard

Today is the birthday of thrifty Zachary Taylor, twelfth president of the United States. He refused to accept a letter because it had postage due, not realizing it was from his party, offering him the nomination to run for president. Happy Birthday, Zach!

Today I will pay whatever postage is due.

November 25

So Near and Yet So Far

Happiness is having a large, loving, close-knit family in another city.
—George Burns

It's easy to imagine your family is perfect when they live somewhere else. With enough time and distance, families look much more loveable, and so do you. So near and yet so far is just the right distance.

Today I will encourage my relatives to move to another city,
so we can become a more perfect family.

November 26

Poignant Memories

I don't like nostalgia unless it's mine.
—Lou Reed

Other people's slide shows, videos, picture albums, and walks down memory lane are not the same as yours. They're not as thrilling, not as fascinating, not as profound, not as memorable. You had to be there.

Today I'll take only my dog for a stroll down memory lane.

November 27

SURVIVAL OF THE FITTEST

Anything can happen to me tomorrow,
But at least nothing more can happen to me yesterday.
—Ashleigh Brilliant

Yesterday is over. You survived. What a miracle. By tomorrow, today will be over. Another miracle. Yesterday was less than perfect. Today will be imperfect in ways you can't even imagine. Tomorrow will have to take care of itself.

When today is less than perfect,
I will remember that I survived yesterday.

November 28

ADVICE AND CONSENT

I have found that the best way to give advice to your children is
to find out what they want and then advise them to do it.
—Harry S. Truman

When you encourage children or adults to do just what they want to do anyway, they will think that you are wise, insightful, and clever. Many excellent reputations belong to people who know exactly how to do this.

Today I will expand my sphere of influence
by being uncharacteristically supportive.

November 29

You Snooze, You Lose

You've been sleeping for years, waiting for the handsome prince to kiss you and wake you from your dreams. Better you should set your alarm clock.
— Enid Howarth and Jan Tras

Snow White taught you how to care for the men in your life even when they're grumpy, sleepy, sneezy, or dopey. You've worked hard, been patient, played dead, preserved yourself under glass, and dreamed of being rescued. It's time to wake up.

Today I will rise from my glass coffin, stretch, yawn, and kick butt.

November 30

Quitting Once More

The only way to stop smoking is to just stop—no ifs, ands, or butts.
— Edith Zittler

Humorist Mark Twain, the author of *Tom Sawyer, Life on the Mississippi, Huckleberry Finn,* and other American classics, was born on this date in 1835. A committed cigar smoker, he said that quitting smoking was easy; he'd done it hundreds of times.

Today I will enjoy quitting one more time.

December 1

BREAKING THE RULES

Courage is grace under pressure.
—Ernest Hemingway

On this day in 1955 in Montgomery, Alabama, Rosa Parks was arrested for refusing to give up her seat and move to the back of a municipal bus. Her arrest triggered a boycott of the Montgomery bus system. Rosa Parks' courageous act marked the birth of the civil rights movement and the death of segregation in the South.

Today I will be courageously outrageous and do the right thing.

December 2

SHOP AND DROP

I never think that people die. They just go to department stores.
—Andy Warhol

Just before the holidays, shopping malls become a little like heaven, a little like hell. Star-studded and filled with celestial music, they are crammed with people happy to trample you in their quest for the perfect gift. Move aside. A department store is not a good place to die.

Today I will not shop till I drop.

December 3

TIME WARP

Warning: Dates in calendar are closer than they appear.
–Author Unknown

Life is moving faster than you are. You're the tortoise and life is the hare. Yesterday it was summer. You blinked, and today it's December. It's always later than you think.

Today I will fast-forward my mind and
try to catch up with the rest of the world.

December 4

KEYS TO SUCCESS

Success is simply a matter of luck. Ask any failure.
–Earl Wilson

Success isn't simply anything; it's a very complicated something. It means being in the right place at the right time, having all the necessary skills and tools, all the planets perfectly aligned, tons of good fortune, and practice, baby, practice.

Today I will become one with my successes and my failures.

December 5

TRUE CONFESSIONS

The office of president is such a bastardized thing, half royalty and half democracy, that nobody knows whether to genuflect or spit.
—Jimmy Breslin

On this day in 1876, President Ulysses S. Grant acknowledged his mistakes in an unprecedented speech of apology to Congress. He claimed that the serious blunders he'd made while president were not intentionally malicious, but were due only to his inexperience. His errors, he said, were "errors of judgment, not intent."

Today I will grant myself a presidential pardon
for my inexperience and errors of judgment.

December 6

EXPLOSIVE ERROR

*now and then / there is a person born / who is so unlucky
that he runs into accidents / which started to happen / to somebody else.*
—Don Marquis

On this date in 1917, a Norwegian ship accidentally plowed into a French munitions ship in Halifax, Nova Scotia. Unfortunately, the French ship was carrying thousands of tons of explosives and flammables, which ignited in a massive explosion that killed and wounded thousands of people, destroyed the harbor, and caused an immense tidal wave that washed much of the city out to sea.

Today I'll avoid bumping into anything or anyone that might explode.

December 7

FIGHTING WORDS

Speak when you are angry—and you'll make the best speech you'll ever regret.
—Henry Ward Beecher

Fire away. People will remember your pointed barbs, your venomous attacks, your prickly humor, your deadly wit. Your passion will make up for your lack of insight. For this one glorious outburst, you may be punished for the rest of your life. It could be worth it.

Today I will just say it, and then emigrate to Australia.

December 8

GETTING SERIOUS

The one serious conviction that a man should have
is that nothing is to be taken too seriously.
—Nicholas Murray Butler

You tried being serious and keeping a straight face. That didn't work. You tried to be perfect. That certainly didn't work. Now, take on the serious business of living a happy and frivolous life. That might work.

Today I will enjoy the humor in my human condition.

December 9

Breathing Hard

I can remember when the air was clean and sex was dirty.
                                        —George Burns

Once upon a time, no one talked about sex or the air. Now, everyone talks about how both have become dangerous to your health. It wouldn't be easy to give up sex. It would be even harder to give up air.

Today, no matter what the consequences,
I will continue to breathe hard and deep.

December 10

Psychobabble

To err is dysfunctional, to forgive co-dependent.
                                        —Berton Averre

You can't win. Everything you do, think, or feel is labeled to make you anxious about your mental health. In truth, being normal just means muddling through your imperfect life with grace, love, luck, and a sense of humor.

Today I will use my old psychology text as a doorstop.

December 11

FEAR OF FLAWING

Without my personality flaws, I would have no personality at all.
                                        –Enid Howarth and Jan Tras

You were born with an invisible label giving instructions for care. It said: "Any flaws in your human fabric are an integral part of the weave. Variations in shading and texture only enhance the quality of the design. Wash gently with mild soap and water; do not use bleach; do not tumble dry." Follow the directions.

Today I will overcome my fear of flawing.

December 12

OVER AND OVER UNTIL IT'S OVER

It is not true that life is one damn thing after another—
it's the same damn thing over and over.
                                        –Edna St. Vincent Millay

Same old, same old. You've been through this before, and many times before that. Welcome to yesterday and the day before. You'll be here again tomorrow and probably the day after. It's the same damn thing over and over, just like the poet says.

Today I will play it again, Sam.

December 13

CLASSY ENEMIES

Money couldn't buy friends, but you got a better class of enemy.
–Spike Milligan

High-class enemies usually dress better, eat better, drive better cars, and use more expensive drugs than you do. Why settle for less?

Today I will upgrade my lifestyle
and exchange my poor enemies for rich ones.

December 14

FEELING FORTY

Forty is the old age of youth; fifty the youth of old age.
–Victor Hugo

If you're under forty, forty seems like the end of excitement. If you remember being forty, you know it was just the beginning. Perspective is everything.

Today I will look kindly on being forty no matter how old I am.

December 15

TEACHING TOOLS

I'll make the mistakes. Someone else can learn from them.
–Enid Howarth and Jan Tras

Your mistakes are your gift to future generations. They could be a teaching tool, a whole curriculum. Required Courses: Foolish Choices 101; Faux Pas 202; Bloopers 303; Ineffective Coping Skills for Graduate Credit Only. Register early.

Today I will make mistakes that the entire world can learn from.

December 16

HEARING AIDS

Without music, life would be a mistake.
–Friedrich Nietzsche

Celebrate! Today is Beethoven's birthday! He began losing his hearing before he was thirty. Miraculously, he continued to create and conduct some of the world's greatest and most joyous music. In 1824, although totally deaf, he premiered his Ninth Symphony and heard neither his music nor the thunderous applause.

Today I will honor Beethoven and turn a deaf ear to my limitations.

December 17

MAN WILL NEVER FLY DAY

You won't skid if you stay in a rut.
−Frank McKinney Hubbard

On this date in 1903, Orville and Wilbur Wright made history. At Kitty Hawk, North Carolina, they flew the first powered airplane. They were off the ground for less than a minute. Despite this monumental feat, and all the aviation history since, the Man Will Never Fly Society continues to meet annually on December 16 to celebrate its motto, "Birds fly, men drink."

Today I will drink like a bird and fly like a man.

December 18

MISSION CONTROL

Trying to control the universe would probably work best if you were God.
−Enid Howarth and Jan Tras

Trying to organize the cosmos is a lonely and thankless job. Most people don't appreciate that you're always right and only want what's best for them. Despite everything you do, opinions clash, comets collide, fruit rots, arches fall. Leave mission control in more capable and experienced hands.

Today I will only take on what's humanly possible.

December 19

DIET-CRAZED

Jack Sprat could eat no fat,
His wife could eat no lean.
A real sweet pair of neurotics.
—Jack Sharkey

Diet today. Eat saltines and drink gallons of water. By tonight you will be seriously hungry, lightheaded, and depressed. Make yourself suffer for all those years of pizza, milkshakes, and fries. When you are really starving, cheat.

Today I will not let my diet turn me into a fruitcake.

December 20

UNDERDOG DAY

We can't all be heroes because someone has to
sit on the curb and clap as they go by.
—Will Rogers

This day celebrates all underdogs and unsung heroes. Without the workers behind the scenes, it would be a different scene altogether. Consider Sherlock Holmes without Dr. Watson, Robinson Crusoe without Friday, the Lone Ranger without Tonto, Rocky without Bullwinkle.

Today I will thank those heroes who loyally stand by me,
cheer me on, and back me up.

December 21

WINTER SOLSTICE

Thank heavens, the sun has gone in, and I don't have to go out and enjoy it.
—Logan Pearsall Smith

The first day of winter is the shortest day of the year and thus the longest night of the year. In the Northern Hemisphere it's the beginning of winter. In the Southern Hemisphere it's the beginning of summer. It's an upside-down, right-side-up kind of day.

Tonight I will take the longest nap of the year.

December 22

HOLIDAY WEIGH-IN

Never weigh more than your refrigerator.
—Barbara Johnson

Unless you are broader than a barn, eat, drink, and be merry. Unless you weigh more than your refrigerator, enjoy the bounty of the season. Restraint is for wimps.

Today I will weigh my refrigerator and be glad.

December 23

THE MANY FACES OF CHRISTMAS

There are some people who want to throw their arms around you
simply because it is Christmas; there are other people who want
to strangle you simply because it is Christmas.
–Robert Lynd

Christmas brings out the best and the worst in everyone. Some create uncondi-tional love and flaming plum pudding. Some create confusion and inedible fruit-cakes. Some create nothing and flee to the beaches in Samoa. You exhibit all, some, and none of the above tendencies. 'Tis the season.

Today I will resist strangling anyone simply because it's Christmas.

December 24

ANNUAL VISITATION

Santa Claus has the right idea: visit people once a year.
–Victor Borge

On your annual holiday visit, make Santa your model. Arrive on time. Bring lots of gifts and good cheer. Share the milk and cookies. Be jovial, but don't wear the lampshade on your head. Clean up after yourself and your reindeer. Dash away, leaving a trail of peace, joy, and good will.

Just for today I will be the perfect guest.

December 25

SELECTIVE YULETIDE MEMORIES

The perfect holiday won't happen this year. But then it never has.
                                    –Enid Howarth and Jan Tras

You only remember the good holiday stuff. You forget the times the dog threw up on the rug, the kids fought over the toys and drew blood, the tree caught fire, the relatives got drunk and slept at the dinner table. Your selective memory ain't what it used to be, but then it never was.

Today I will abandon my memory of the perfect holiday
and embrace reality with courage and mistletoe.

December 26

BEGINNING OF KWANZAA

Holidays are often overrated disturbances of routine, costly and uncomfort-able, and they usually need another holiday to correct their ravages.
                                    –E.V. Lucas

For many African-Americans in the United States, Kwanzaa is a welcome alter-native to the commercialism of the holiday season. Kwanzaa, the beginning of a traditional African harvest festival, stresses unity of the family and the virtues of honor, compassion, and community. The word *Kwanzaa* means *first fruit*.

Today I will dig myself out from under the tinsel and holly,
and enjoy the fruits of the season.

December 27

ONE YEAR AT A TIME

Year, n. A period of three hundred and sixty-five disappointments.
—Ambrose Bierce

It's been a long time since January. Some things have gone your way. Some haven't. There have been surprises, delights, and disappointments. It's been a year to forget, a year to remember.

Today I will prepare myself for another year
of foolish and misguided expectations.

December 28

TANGO WITH CHANGE

Any change, even a change for the better,
is always accompanied by drawbacks and discomforts.
—Arnold Bennett

Changes are rarely easy, smooth, or well choreographed. Most change involves one step forward, two steps backward, three to the left, and cha-cha-cha. Expect to stumble, sweat, and step on a few toes, including your own.

Today I will tango with change
and resist my urge to flee from the dance floor.

December 29

COLOR CODING

Traffic signals in New York are just rough guidelines.
—David Letterman

Red usually means stop. Green usually means go. Yellow can mean slow down or go like hell. Depending on where you are, signals can mean anything or nothing at all. It's best to look both ways and pray.

Today I will cross on the green, not in between,
and hope nobody's colorblind.

December 30

CELEBRATING YOURSELF

Sometimes I sing so pretty I make myself cry.
—Jimmy Durante

You've almost made it through another imperfect year. Congratulate yourself for being talented, terrific, and tenacious. Remember all the good deeds you did this year, all the senseless acts of kindness, all the moments of generosity and nobility. Give yourself flowers, applause, gold stars. Cry.

Today I will shower my imperfect self with tears and abundant praise.

December 31

OUT WITH THE OLD

*Middle age is when you're faced with two temptations
and you choose the one that will get you home by 9 o'clock.*
                                                    –Ronald Reagan

Let the children ring in the new year. Let the young folks dance until dawn. You've already done that more times than you can count. Now you can go home, relax, put on your flannel jammies, drink warm milk, and party down to the soothing strains of Guy Lombardo.

Tonight I will be the first on my block to ring in the new year.